Sally Bongers is a film director, photographer and cinematographer, based in Sydney. Sally studied at the Australian Film Television and Radio School, subsequently winning two AFI Awards for Cinematography. She runs her own film production company, *Light Corporation* in Australia. Sally's spiritual journey has taken her from Muktananda to UG Krishnamurti, Ramesh Balsekar to 'Sailor' Bob Adamson and Tony Parsons.

everyday enlightenment

seven stories of awakening

compiled and edited by
Sally Bongers

NON-DUALITY PRESS

First published July 2008 by Non-Duality Press

Typeset in Rotis Semi-Serif & Garth Graphic 11/13
Cover photograph and layout by Sally Bongers and Paul Elliott

Non-Duality Press, Salisbury, SP2 8JP
United Kingdom.

ISBN 978-0-9558290-3-1

www.non-dualitybooks.com

contents

foreword

The falling away of everything. The death of what we take to be 'the little self' and a plunge into something vaster – and more obvious – than the mind could ever hope to grasp. An end to seeking, an end to suffering, an end to the idea that I'm a person in the world. Awakening. Enlightenment. Liberation. It can happen, and it does happen. And yet, it never happens to anyone.

Confused? You should be! The mind could never hope to grasp the ungraspable. But undeniably these shifts, for want of a better word, can and do occur, and from the dawn of human history there has been an ongoing fascination with so-called 'enlightened beings' who have apparently reached this state of absolute release.

But of course, it's not a state at all, and no person has ever awakened. As this wonderful little book will show you, this awakening, or seeing, or whatever you want to call it, does not depend on what you've done, or not done, in the past. Which is to say, it doesn't depend on the person at all, because the person doesn't even exist. But really this is the last thing that a mind hungry for a future awakening wants to hear. It wants awakening for itself, it wants to grasp it, to own it, to possess it, and then to go round the world proclaiming how wonderfully enlightened it is. And so it could never accept that there's nothing it can do, or not do, to get it.

But don't worry, this can never be understood on an intellectual level. And yet when the seeking ends, when the struggle collapses, when 'you' are no longer there, what these words are pointing to is seen in absolute clarity. And then what is revealed is ... well, it's beyond words. But if we have to use words (and words are useful when writing a foreword!) it goes something like this:

In the absence of seeking, what is revealed is Oneness. And in Oneness, life is already complete, and what's more, it's seen that life was always complete, right from the beginning. And at the root of a lifetime of seeking was always the assumption that life wasn't complete, that there was an individual separate from the Whole, that Oneness was out there and not here, that it existed in the so-called 'future'. And out of this assumption, in a million different ways the individual tried to reach completion, and turned to drink or drugs or meditation, but really it was all just a manifestation of the same desire: the desire to return to the Source. But of course the individual could never find the Source, because the individual was already a perfect expression of the Source. That's why the seeking can, and does, go on for a lifetime. What we're looking for is already staring us in the face, but we can't see it, because we're too busy looking for it!

But what can happen, and what the people in this book describe beautifully, in their own words, is the falling away of the seeking, the falling away of the sense of being a separate individual. And in that falling away, the ordinary things of the world reveal their secret, and the secret doesn't look anything like you thought it would. It's beyond religion, beyond ideology, beyond belief, beyond even the ideas of 'awakening' and 'enlightenment'. It's free. It's unconditional. It's so present that anything we say about it just burns up. It's got nothing to do with your goals, your achievements, your desires, your regrets, your spiritual accomplishments, your material failures. It's got nothing to do with you at all. It's here and it's now, and it cannot be found in any future. It's the Open Secret, as Tony Parsons calls it, and it's so well hidden that it appears as everything, literally everything, and yet we still cannot see it.

I love this book because it brings this awakening right back down to earth, and emphasises its ordinariness, an emphasis that seems to be missing in a lot of the current spiritual literature. These seven stories remind us that this seeing is available anywhere, at any time. It doesn't matter how old or young you are, how educated you are, how spiritually aware you are, how big or small or short or tall you are. All of that is rendered meaningless in the seeing that 'you' are just a presently-arising story.

It's the release that can happen in the midst of the messiness of human life. Jesus knew this. At the heart of the cross, in the midst of the most intense suffering known to man, there it was: Eternal Life. Right in the midst of it all – taking the kids to school, being shouted at by your boss, walking in the park, sitting on the toilet – it can be seen: already, nobody is living your life. Already, nobody takes the kids to school, nobody is shouted at by the boss, nobody walks in the park and nobody goes to the toilet. Already, life lives itself, effortlessly. Already, at the heart of life, there is a clarity that the separate individual could never grasp. It's the crucifixion and the resurrection all in one, and it's constantly happening.

Ultimately of course (and here's where the poor little mind gets really confused!) there is no awakening, no liberation, no enlightenment at all. There is just this – what's presently happening. Just present sights, sounds, smells, thoughts. As the old Zen master Fa-ch'ang whispered on his deathbed "Just this, and nothing more." And so really anything we say about awakening isn't true, because in talking about it we've already made it into a 'thing' and killed it. But as Lao-Tzu knew, although the Tao cannot be told, there's no reason why you shouldn't try. After all, when the separate self is gone, what else is there to do?

These seven stories once and for all destroy the myth that enlightenment is something reserved for 'special' people. They expose the fallacy that awakening can be owned by masters, transmitted by gurus... or even taught by teachers! Yes, these are dangerous stories to read. They may just destroy your concepts of awakening and enlightenment ("If you meet the Buddha on the road, kill him.") They may just reveal the secret, right where you are.

Jeff Foster
Brighton, UK
June 2008

introduction

The inspiration for this book started while researching a documentary film I am making called *The Enlightenment Project*.

I was searching for 'enlightened' people, people who had awakened, become liberated, realised, developed 'seeing' – however you want to describe it – people who have had a profound and lasting shift in their realisation of what they are.

My initial interviews were with established teachers and authors, but I soon realised that if we continue to predominantly hear these people talking about 'realisation', it is easy to get the impression that 'realisation' only happens to people like that. I felt that surely there must be *unknown* people out there living with this understanding in the community – and of course, there are.

I eventually found a number of people who still lived their life much as they had done before the realisation, working and living in the everyday world. I have chosen seven of their stories for this book.

They don't use the precise words of non-duality 'teachers' and their stories are filtered through the personality and flavour of each person, which brings an accessible quality that helps convey 'that', that is 'flavourless'.

Hearing these people talk about living with this understanding in the real world (not in an ice-cave somewhere!) confirms the closeness of it all. I realise now that this can 'happen' to anyone. There are no qualifications.

I didn't want the book to become a list of amazing enlightenment experiences, as I am aware of the problems that this can create in the seeker's mind, but in the end I felt that these experiences were a part of the whole picture and needed to be included.

This book can't give you what enlightenment is, but maybe it can show you how close it is to what you already are right now, with no changes needed.

I would like to thank Julian Noyce for his encouragement and support and Tony Parsons, Joan Tollifson, Alan Mann, Victoria Ritchie and Rose Youd for their help. For transcriptions, thanks to Carolyn Samuel and Tania Davies.

I would especially like to thank all the people who kindly agreed to be interviewed and, for his editing and generous spirit, I would like to thank my partner, Paul Elliott.

Sally Bongers
Colo River, Australia
May 2008

end of story

D.A. I'm always very loathe to get too heavily into the story of D. because it doesn't exist really. It's just a fantasy being cooked up right now. And so I very rarely think about it and I don't keep track of what's happened in what year.

I am forty-four years old. I was born in the North East. My father was an engineer and he worked for ICI. I don't think I actually liked the North East very much. The family moved over to the North West when I was five and that's where it feels like home. I grew up there, really enjoyed it and went to the University of York, did a music degree, then some professional playing and composing.

I'd always been interested in Zen and yoga and meditation. I presume it started when I was sixteen or seventeen. I was living outside Manchester and they had a very good library. I decided to start at '000' in the Dewey Decimal System. Luckily '000' is the philosophy section! I started reading through that and came across books on yoga. I took some of them home. They were talking about this thing called 'enlightenment'. It sounded so amazing! I thought: "Why isn't everyone in the world going full out to try and get this thing? It sounds incredible!" I did a bit of mucking around at home, trying meditation techniques. This was back in the seventies when everyone was doing Transcendental Meditation. My mum and dad both tried TM but didn't really get on with it. I was reading lots of Zen, doing as much meditation as I could, experimenting with things.

I never really stuck to one tradition for long. I was very lazy. I still am. I didn't spend twenty years in a Zen monastery ... *(laughter)* ... or ten years or even one year. I just did *one weekend* in France! But I was lucky. I used to live in Finsbury Park and there was a Tibetan Buddhist centre just around the corner, so for about three years I went there regularly. I think that was the longest I've ever spent with any particular religious group.

A first major thing was going to a Douglas Harding summer retreat – an amazing experience. I remember coming back to work after the retreat and moving at half my usual speed, beaming at everyone who I recognised as 'being myself'. It was all happening. All the tears of joy and love and all that bullshit. But after a few weeks, all that faded and I was back to square one. Still reading my books on Zen, still the same.

There were plenty of blissful ecstatic states that came up occasionally – these ecstatic things that come from reading one passage in a book or maybe hearing some great music – and, of course, I went through the whole idiocy of thinking: "Oh wow! I've got it! This is wonderful, this is amazing, this is it! I'm enlightened!".

And then two days later it's gone, and you think: "Oh, damn!" You get tired of it. You think: "Well this is all rubbish. I don't want a temporary experience."

And then nothing really interesting happened until 2000 when I first went to a Tony Parsons' meeting. I was totally blown away. It was very, very joyful and ecstatic. Then I went to Nathan Gill's meetings and Roger Linden's and that was it! (*laughter*) End of story. (*laughter*)

I remember that very first meeting. At the end, Tony Parsons came up and hugged me. I couldn't really say anything. I just kept on going to every single meeting. As Tony says: "All I'm doing is reminding you of what you already know." So in the back of my mind, I'd always suspected that this was how things were but you're gradually conditioned away from that seeing. To hear someone stand up in front of you and tell you what you already know about how things are, then there's this big joy: "Oh yes, yes, yes! I was right, I was right, I was right all the time. All the time I thought I was wrong and mad. No, it's true!" So, yeah, I kept going to Tony for a bit. Then the ecstatic things gradually faded away. It all became flat and normal and, you know, so so. I think that was the big turning point.

I was in a kind of dead zone in 2004. I read loads of non-duality books and went to loads of Tony Parsons' meetings, went to loads of Nathan Gill's meetings, went to Roger Linden's meetings – but that was more of a kind of entertainment, something to do and something I was interested in. I didn't sit at home desperately trying to figure it out: "How can I do this? How can I get it? What is it that I'm missing?" I didn't think about it at all. I just let it all wash over. There came a point where I understood it all, you know? Total intellectual understanding, no problem at all – but you know that it still hasn't happened. And you know there's nothing you can do. You drag yourself along to yet more meetings. It's like being dead.

I had a girlfriend who got it four months ahead of me. It was bloody annoying. She had a phenomenal intellect and a very, very sharp mind. Whereas I'd been going to these Tony and Roger meetings for four years, she just came down and within about six weeks, it's all over. All very clearly seen. She was lumbered with a boyfriend who still hadn't got it, this idiot who was still going to non-duality meetings. (*laughter*) She refused to go to them anymore: "God, I'd rather cut my own head off than go to another bloody non-duality meeting!"

Do you want to hear the dramatic 'enlightenment' story? (*laughter*) Well, I think maybe the most important thing that happened prior to the 'big event' was just failure in lots of areas of life. I was in a really dark depressed state because everything had fallen away. My degree was in music composition and, back in the early 1980's, I still had the delusion that you could earn a living as a professional composer, writing hardcore classical music. I gradually saw the commissions becoming fewer and fewer and eventually the day came when I just couldn't pay the rent. So there was professional failure on the one hand and then romantic failures and money failure. The whole house of cards was collapsing.

It was the summer of 2004. I mean, in retrospect, it was all arranged quite perfectly. I was desperately in love with a girl and we were sort of living together. She dumped me. That was just the last straw. Everything else had gone but she was the light in my life. Then that light was blown out: *"Boom"*. There was nothing left. Just this big black hole of depression. I was absolutely distraught – but being a typical male I repressed it and thought: "OK, I'm fine, I'll find someone else. I don't need her". I stomped off and repressed almost all memory of her.

I think it was about a month later that Wayne Liquorman came over to do a talk in London. I went and she was there as well. Seeing her again, suddenly all that grief and misery came up – *whoompf!* I realised what I was missing. And so we spoke for about half an hour that day and then she went off. For the next few weeks, I was really, really, *really* low.

I went to Roger Linden's weekend. All the way through, I was really miserable and depressed and getting worse by the day. Luckily, we'd arranged to have a one-to-one on the following Monday. All we did was therapy. Roger got me to feel all the misery and despair and to let it all out. Right towards the end, we spoke a tiny bit about non-duality. He was talking about the witness. I think from reading lots of Douglas Harding books and going to lots of his retreats I'd got into this trap of imagining that the witness was something standing just behind and above me, kind of localised back there. I remember Roger said to me: "No, no. Everything is the witness!" Suddenly, something clicked. Roger could see that something had happened. He looked at me and said: "Yes, but there's still duality, isn't there?" I said: "Oh yes, absolutely". He said: "Let's have another one-to-one."

The following Friday, I can't remember what Roger said. It was the usual chat. Then he said: "Let's just pause." I closed my eyes and rested there and *"phoom!"* Everything disappeared. After a while, I opened my eyes and he asked: "How was it?" I said: "I can't say."

I think it was totally beyond words. In a sense, absolutely nothing happened and that's what was so extraordinary. The self image fell away. The habitual idea of yourself gradually faded away until there was just what is seen, hanging there in nothingness, in emptiness.

Roger asked a few questions to check me out and see if it was really clear, making sure there weren't any sort of blind spots. Then he asked: "Well, have you got what you came for?" (*laughter*) I said: "Yes. Thank you!" (*laughter*) and we shook hands (*laughter*) and I staggered down the road, utterly blown away.

D. had disappeared and there was just this emptiness walking down the road. Luckily, I wasn't working at the time and I was living in this very nice flat on the banks of the Thames, so I spent the next four or five days sitting by the river doing absolutely nothing, just staring, staring blankly, just watching the Thames flowing by, just watching the trees and the birds and the sun on the water and not actually thinking this but sort of having the feeling: "Oh, thank God. Yeah, thank fuck it's all over". And it all sort of became clear.

❊　　❊　　❊

When the seeking fell away, it was massive, enormous really – not only psychological but physical as well. There was a massive dropping of tension and enormous peace. Other people noticed that something had changed. After I came back from that fateful meeting with Roger, my flatmate, a devoted practitioner of Tibetan Buddhism, looked at me. She had an idea of what had happened.

For me, it wasn't a bliss thing actually. It wasn't really bliss. It was release and a massive sigh of relief. It was peace. And then it settled back to normality – everything as it is. But, thank God, without that insane seeking. I often say: "It's like you've had a really bad fever, you've had some tropical disease for forty years and you've been delirious and in bed, thrashing around desperately. Then one morning, you wake up and the fever's gone. You're not delirious anymore. You go down to the shops and buy some milk and that's it. It's back to normality after the lunacy." And once that core assumption of separation has been seen through, that's it. It's seen through. It's finished.

The extraordinary special 'experience' is gone, you know, like all experiences go. Faded away. Gone completely. I was lucky that I didn't fall into the trap of thinking the extreme experience was 'it'. Luckily, I knew: "No. What 'it' is is just 'isness'. Just what *is* is what everyone's been searching for – which is mad! It's insane because there is only what is."

What actually happens when the seeking stops is just the realisation of 'isness'. It's not an experience. It's: "Oh, so it's just this". And this never goes away. It doesn't matter what experience comes – whether it's boredom or being hungover or having a headache. All kinds of stupidities can still come up, of course, and still do – selfish, ignorant behaviour, almost any kind of stupidity you can think of – being lazy, not tidying up at home, not wanting to wash dishes. Every kind of human weakness is still there.

❊   ❊   ❊

So I mean OK, the spiritual thing is sorted. Spiritual seeking has stopped, yes, absolutely. So seeking does end – but only *spiritual* seeking. There can still be seeking for money, most definitely. Wanting a wife, wanting a flat, wanting all the usual things, that all goes on. Maybe a bit less obsessively. Just on the backburner.

There's more ease now – but there are still problems. Hassles with money and health and relationships and everything – especially relationships. Most of the suffering comes from the incessant thinking about it, and there's less of that than there was before. I think there can be different degrees of falling away of habitual thinking, I think it's different for different people. But problems are still problems. You still fall in love with the most inappropriate people and make an absolute fool of yourself and then get really upset if they dump you – just like anyone else. Just normal life really.

There's an increased ability to stand back from thinking and not be enslaved by it. It's different for different people. Some carry on not really caring how much involvement and thinking there is, because it's true: "It doesn't make any difference." I mean, oneness is oneness, awareness is awareness – so you can think as much as you like. Nevertheless, once you've seen how much suffering the thinking is causing, then for me at least, it's rather a good idea to drop it – unless you're a masochist! There's no big difference in the nature of thinking, just slightly less tendency to identify and get totally lost in clouds of thought, which grab you and drag you into a story. That's all.

At the same time, there is the view: "Look, there is only oneness. There is only awareness, so it doesn't matter". 'Caught-upness' is fine, being totally lost in the clouds of suffering created by thoughts is fine. It's all oneness. It doesn't matter – which is true.

People often confuse certain kinds of behaviour with liberation. Say if someone has trained to be a therapist for decades, they develop these ways of being with people, ways of relating, being very attentive to people, being present, being calm and serene. It has absolutely nothing to do with liberation. People confuse those characteristics as being a sign of an enlightened human being, whereas they're a sign of having done therapy training. I'm not sure if there are any signs of liberation really, apart from being a bit more relaxed and at ease.

❊   ❊   ❊

If we're looking straight forward, we can't actually see much of the body. There's a mental image – a self image – which provides the image of the body and that locates the sense of me. If that mental image disappears, then it can be seen that there's actually no one here. In my case, it was a quite literal disappearance of the body actually. It was accompanied by a massive sinking of the centre of gravity. It felt like the centre of gravity had fallen down to my ankles. It was absolutely physical.

So there's a massive relaxation and a dropping of everything – but that was only an experience – so, of course, it went. This is only what's happened to D. For other people, they don't have anything like that. They have their own thing. It's completely different. For other people it can just be a sort of very simple understanding – with no apparent shade of experience.

All that's found is awareness, which always is, which everyone has. It's not a special state. It's just: "This – here – now – is – awareness." There's nothing special. It's just awareness.

The classic mistake that people make is mistaking an experience for liberation, so they can have an experience which lasts six minutes or six days or six years and they're absolutely sure that they've got it and then the experience goes away and they say: "Oh, no! I've lost it now!" and they are all depressed. That's the most classic mistake.

Experiences and sensations and thoughts come up and then they go away. There's an assumption that it's 'me' thinking this and it's 'me' having these emotions – but it's only an assumption. In fact, everyone is in the same state. Things are coming and then going. There's no big deal. There's no big difference. It's recognising what is *already* the case for everyone – that there isn't a 'me' or an 'I' controlling things. It's just things happening.

I think 'not getting caught up so much in thought-storms' is something which happens gradually for most people. There's a gradual 'dis-identification' from that kind of thing. I actually think it's quite important not to keep getting caught up in the thought–storm because it does cause so much suffering – those habitual clouds of thought which grab you and drag you into a story. At the same time, there is the view: "Look, there is only oneness. There is only awareness, so it doesn't matter." 'Caught-upness' is fine, being totally lost in the clouds of suffering created by thoughts is fine. It's all oneness. It doesn't matter – which is true.

* * *

It's funny. There are all sorts of unconscious assumptions people have about how it will be different when liberation happens. One of them which is very, very common is the assumption that uncomfortable sensations in the body will be replaced by joyful, blissful, easeful feelings – but, no, no, it's the same. They're just feelings.

If anything's changed it's that the mental image of my body and the picture of what it's like has gone. Instead there are just sensations and colours.

One major thing that changes is that the mental model of how the world is falls away – the self image, the idea of a world, troops fighting in Iraq – all that kind of stuff falls away. There's just coffee cups, a table, a microphone ...

The whole political thing is a dream. I mean you can still participate in the dream. I went on the anti-war march before the Iraq War began, the two million people march in London, and that's just what happens. At the same time, there isn't any Iraq. Any kind of action can come up as appropriate but there's not the insane avoidance of clarity by constantly worrying: "Oh, but what about Iraq? What about Afghanistan?" Constantly running away from here and now into thinking about what isn't here and now. It's an avoidance mechanism.

Some people will be active and others won't. If I hear someone at a non-duality meeting ask a question: "Oh, but what about all the people being killed in Iraq?" the main reason they're asking that is they're desperate *not* to investigate what is actually going on – whether they actually exist and what the nature of their own life is. The best way of avoiding confronting that is to run off into some idea: "Oh, but what about Afghanistan?" or "What about this?" or "What about that?"

✳   ✳   ✳

People generate fantasies about what it's like. There's a famous photo of Ramana Maharshi which everyone has seen. From that one photo, people build up a fantasy of what his life was like and what he was like as a person. In fact, there are loads of other photos in which he seems absolutely pissed off and bored and insane. If people saw those photos, they'd have a completely different image of what Ramana Maharshi was like.

I've got a friend who flies around the world teaching non-duality. He uses Douglas Harding exercises. They're very good techniques to give people an initial flash, an initial glimpse. I think they become a trap after that because it's constantly giving people the idea that there's some special state or something you can do through some meditative practice, whereas you don't need any practice or any technique because there is only awareness - right here, right now. So why do a practice? There's only 'isness' or 'thisness'. Why do a practice to generate some alternate state when this is it already?

✳   ✳   ✳

I think everything's pretty much the same as before. Generally, I'm sort of easygoing and a fairly polite guy - but if someone's really boring I'll probably get up and walk away. One change can be the freedom to let the inner bastard or the inner bitch out. A girlfriend I had always repressed her inner bitch due to religious upbringing. When liberation happened, it came out full force! If she wanted to say something rude to someone, she would say it, *wham*, full out! It was a tremendous relief and a joyful freedom for her to be able, at last, to be rude if she felt like it. And other people have said that as well. I know one or two people who on certain occasions will be really direct and rude - because there's a freedom to do that

Everything carries on as normal but without the confusion. I remember on that fateful day talking to Roger when this had happened and he asked me to try and describe what it was like, what the difference was? I interlinked the fingers of my hands and said: "Previously, all the thoughts were a tangled mass like that, and slowly they just all unfurled." The hands are open and everything's seen clearly as it is, without the entanglement. There's not the mental confusion - but all the programming carries on.

In the year after liberation, there was this gradual process of belief in the personal story falling away. About a year afterwards that process seemed to have completed. It was a really nice feeling to have dropped the past, a really beautiful lightness. It's wonderful. People are always worrying about losing their memory and I think: "For Godsake, lose it as quickly as possible. It's shit." It's wonderful not having a memory.

People often give lip service to the ideas: "There's *only* the present. There is no past. There is no future." But they don't actually mean it. Slowly, you actually, *really* realise that there isn't a past. If you're talking about your childhood, you really are cooking up a fantasy in the present – which has no reality whatsoever. This is the present and these things are happening. But anything else is just an idea, it's a fantasy. Present experience is clear and obvious, but we still have these assumptions that something happened or something will happen but in fact that's never the case. There's only – *(snaps fingers)*. People often talk about being aware moment to moment, being aware now – now – now. But there's only *one* now.

For quite a time there has been no sense of personal history and it's very, very nice when that personal history drops away. Fantasizing about the past and future has fallen away. Perception seems to change slightly. If the brain activity is not continually engaged in fantasising about pasts and futures then there can be more attention on actual sensory input – seeing, hearing, touching, tasting. There's nothing mystical about it, there's just not so much distraction all the time from what's actually happening. It's just greater clarity. The present becomes a bit brighter and clearer and nicer.

It's very hard to describe. There's just more of an ease with how you are. There's less of the should and shouldn'ts, less of the trying to conform to some model, to some image of how you should be. There's just more ease and lightness. Lots of people notice that after meditating when you open your eyes, everything looks crisper and brighter and clearer – well, it's like that more or less all the time. It's no big deal, no visions of deities or anything – just a bit more clarity.

Roger Linden talks about awareness being aware of itself. Consciousness is kind of startled and amazed at the fact of being conscious. And it's like: "Wow! The actual fact of there being consciousness is so staggering." There could be just blank nothingness. Isn't it amazing that there is the ability to hear and see and touch the table? Just being able to see, being able to hear. It's like the universe is saying: "Wow! How did I get here? How does this happen?" Seeing what is as a miracle.

❋ ❋ ❋

How can you really say what liberation really is? It's just the end of seeking and the end of obsessing about spiritual experiences. I think that's the essential point.

It's like that old Indian metaphor: "The rope of seeking has got to be completely burnt to ashes" – and God knows how long it's going to take – it could be years – but when it's burnt to ashes, that's it. You can't use it as a rope anymore. It's totally fucked. And then

15

you can say: "Thank God, I'm over all that stuff!"

What Ramesh Balsekar says about it is quite encouraging: "You're being dragged along and being made to do what's necessary at any time so you don't need to worry." Everything that's necessary is coming to you and you don't need to worry about struggling or not struggling, or trying or not trying. The universe is providing exactly what you need at every moment, even though you may not like it.

I suppose the only important thing worth saying is: "It's this *now*, you know? It's not some special experience in the future." These teachers who talk about non-duality or enlightenment, all they're doing is accurately describing how it is *now* for everyone. They're not describing some special state that they have attained, which *you* may attain if you're very, very lucky, if you attend enough of their meetings, if you pay enough money. All they're doing is describing how it is now for you – but it can take a while to realise that that's the case.

I like to say just that there is clarity and it's all obvious now. It's obvious that all is consciousness. There is only awareness and then we attach labels to certain images that appear in awareness. We call that one 'table' and call that one 'me'. It's just obvious and clear how it is. That's all.

i am the tree

C.B. I was born in 1939 and raised in Atlanta and New Orleans by Southern parents. There was a lot of hypocrisy then in the South. It was during Segregation, before Blacks had a right to vote. I grew up sceptical and suspicious of authority. I was the rebellious one in the family and my sister was the good one. I was always screwing up. When I was sixteen I ran away from home and had my son when I was seventeen. In Virginia I married a stable guy who was a nice father for my son.

Then I got in touch with a friend who was attending Berkeley University in the sixties and my husband and I decided to go there. We sold our house and bought a school bus, took the seats out and put all of our stuff in it. We had a great time but eventually it turned sour. About that time, the 'back to the land' thing was happening. When my parents died, I bought some land up in Northern California, way back in the woods where we built a homestead and lived.

❊   ❊   ❊

When I was twenty-one, I had an experience of the true nature of reality but I didn't understand what had happened. I was in a dentist's office having some work

17

done and was given nitrous oxide. It felt as if I slipped out of my body and was up on the ceiling looking down at the dentist and his nurse. Then there was a sense of flying out into space, into blackness. I was disembodied, just a point of light. I had everything and it was so joyful and so blissful and perfect. Then they were trying to wake me up and the thought came: "Which body?" I could have come back as a rock or a snail or anything. Then I was on the ceiling again and saw the body in the chair and thought: "That one." I slipped back through the top of my head into the body like a hand into a glove. The nurse and the dentist were looking very distraught but I knew that everything was fine.

It was so profound and yet I couldn't find anything to validate it – until I found acid, which was sometimes pretty close but not it. Too weird. That was before all the books about this came out. I went to the library and started at 'A'. I was going to read every book in there until I found out what had happened because I knew it was true. So that started the search but it was sporadic.

After that initial experience, I started reading books and I found some Buddhist books which said things like: "If you do this for a hundred and twenty years or over many lifetimes, then maybe you will get it." But I knew that it is immediate. It is available now. Perhaps it was part of that rebellious, suspicious attitude I've always had. Also, I think because I was into drugs for so many years, I developed the idea it was 'other than'. Sometimes I would read books that said things like: "It's just listening to the birds and watching the sky," but I thought that sounded really boring. I was sure that couldn't be it. It had to be better.

* * *

At some point later in my life, everything fell apart and got really bad. In 1977, a friend took me by the hand and drove me to see Muktananda, who was in the States on a world tour. I didn't want to go see him, but afterwards I found myself not smoking dope, not drinking wine, and I realised that something had taken place when I met him. I became a devotee and a follower for the next twelve years, getting my basic training. After Baba (Muktananda) died, the whole thing fell apart, but that's when I met Jean Dunn, a devotee of Nisargadatta, who wrote *Consciousness and the Absolute*. She was so normal and ordinary that it was a great awakening for me. I studied with her for about six years as well as with other teachers, including Ramesh Balsekar.

There was a kind of gradual awakening going on over that time. Sometimes I felt I was almost getting it but wasn't sure. The concept of getting it all at once, I felt, was a block because while it was taking place I was waiting for the big bang and blocking what was already there. That is what the story was – this big light would come on and angels would sing or whatever. So it was hard for me to recognise that it was me, it was this, not something else. I had different techniques that I would use to try to bring myself back to this like mantras and just remembering. It seemed helpful and for me it was gradual. The big bang never happened. There was thinking along the lines of: "I'm there, now I'm not there." It was a bit crazy-making. As long as I am playing that game I can't recognise that I am there, that I am that. Gradually it dawned on me that I was playing games and I was full of concepts that were getting in my way and as I let go of those I began to embody the truth of who I am.

* * *

Then Ramesh Balsekar came from India and I went to a retreat with him. I came home from that retreat and said to my friend: "I got it!" After that day, there was still fluctuation so what I got was not the total it. I can't point to any day as 'when it happened'. It was too gradual and fluctuated so much. What I got that day was the realisation that there was nothing to get. I had spent all of these years doing all of these things. I learned Sanskrit, I chanted four hours a day, I meditated four hours a day. I loved it but it was insane. I really thought that I was getting somewhere with all of that stuff. But it is like a process of reprogramming your mind and with some of us that takes quite a while. I had heard it and heard it and heard it from Jean Dunn and other people and I just happened to be with Ramesh on this retreat when I realised that there is nothing to get.

Being a seeker becomes such an identity, such a habit, a way of life with a seeming prestige attached to it. That is another reason, I think, that we keep on with the trip. It becomes a way of life and if it's given up – then what will we do? You can't make an announcement because everyone has these expectations of you being a certain way, so it seems better to just go on seeking. But that day, all of the things I had heard from all these different directions over the years just came together and I got it. I got that there's nothing to get.

But still it felt gradual and seemed to come and go. I went to other teachers: Eckhart Tolle, Francis Lucille, U.G. Krishnamurti. There was a lot of reading and over time it seemed to become more solid and immovable. There wasn't a drifting back and forth. It was more stable. I guess the whole search, the whole path, took about twenty-seven years from the time I met Baba. Then I quit going to teachers and since then I don't like to read any more.

I felt I gained a lot from listening to the teachers I went to but, at a certain point, it is no longer helpful. When you get to your destination, you throw away the map. You are there. You don't need to keep checking back. There is a paradox and both things are true. It is helpful and at some point it is not helpful.

❈ ❈ ❈

Consciousness animates me every day and that is what interests me, not hearing someone else's story, someone else's take on it, but rather how it is manifesting in me. I feel more like me than ever, with that same awareness that you have as a child when you know. You know who you are. I'm happy. I live my life.

It's different than in normal life where you may have a good day and then you have a really bad day. Now it's never that bad because you know that it's just your story. It's like there is something underneath you, holding you, although it's way down. There is a level at which it doesn't bother you. I can get into things with my family and my grandchildren which seem really bad but it's almost like watching it being bad but it's not, really. The identity is not as the person so you can't get swept away like you could before. That is the nature of the shift.

* * *

Sometimes I see shadows on the wall when the sun goes down or I see light coming through the leaves or reflecting off water and I am transfixed by it. I could look at it forever. Artists and poets see that. I don't think it's that extraordinary - just an awareness of beauty.

I didn't really have that before. There was always busy-ness, running from one thing to the other, being caught up with whatever. Even though I have always been out in the country a lot with nature, it is different. You become everything and everything takes on this other quality of there being no separation between you and it. Before I would look at a tree and think, "Isn't that a beautiful tree?" Now, I look at the tree and I am the tree. That's the difference. There's just that oneness.

There is no subject and object. You can feel the leaves, you can smell the smells, you can feel the stickiness of the sap, you can feel the lightness in the breeze. It is more of a complete experience than just looking at it. A poet would say the same. I think when we try to describe this too much it goes away. It's like we beat it to death.

Words can't reach it. They can only point to it. It's so natural and normal that to try to go into some kind of description doesn't make any sense because, unless you are on the exact same level or wave-length, you will misunderstand it. You will understand it through your own understanding.

❊ ❊ ❊

When I came out of the Ashram, I had no marketable skills. I hadn't even finished high school. I didn't want to just go out and get a job so I went back to nursing school at about age forty and graduated when I was forty-five. I didn't want to do mainstream nursing, I never wanted to do mainstream anything. There is a leper colony on one of the islands of Hawaii so I went and worked there for a year. Then I did other off-beat nursing, with AIDS patients in a hospice, and on a mobile hospital bus in India which went around the villages and gave simple medical care to the villagers.

I never put together much money but I didn't really care about money. I just wanted to have a good time and figure it out. I ended up here in this subsidised housing for seniors. It's easy and comfortable and simple and small. My income is $850 a month and my rent is $182 and I have such a good life. It's exciting, I travel, I don't know how I pull it off but I have always done this. I haven't had a lot but always enough to live comfortably and have a fun, exciting life. It's totally great. Life feels good. There is definitely more love, more compassion. There's understanding, patience, joy. The deepest feeling I have is gratitude.

In this whole unravelling, meditation was very, very helpful through those early years. Becoming familiar with who you are without the story. I don't meditate formally now but I do find myself just being very still at any time and many times during the day. I guess you could call that mediation but I see it as more of a preparation, becoming familiar with that place of who we are. Again, once you know, you don't need techniques or practices. You need them early but you don't need them after, I think.

* * *

You don't want to accept the ordinary. It's like: "This can't be it. Is this all there is to it?" That's what keeps you from recognising what it is - the expectation that it is not this, but it's over there somewhere, it's going to get better, brighter - whatever the expectations are, whatever you have been conjuring up in your mind.

Eventually the idea that you haven't got it yet just peters out. Even the thoughts that come up about it are just the story. It's your mind. It doesn't want to lose control. It's not going to let you go so easily. It's going to keep on running, though the fact that you don't believe it takes the juice out of it and weakens it more and more. It will die a natural death.

I'm only talking from this small little place where I'm functioning in the world. If we were in a cave in Tibet and meditated for twenty years or whatever, then we would be having a different experience from what we are having now. My thing was realising this duality and wanting to integrate it. So the second half of my sadhana was a process of integration with what is. The range is as wide as there are people and cultures.

For me, right now, I don't want attendants. I don't

want to be so far gone that I can't function. I can see how that would easily happen if you just had nothing to do all day except be. It's like when you look at a tree or you sit in meditation and you feel that you are so at one with everything you could sit there forever. If there were nothing to pull you out of there, who knows how it would be?

It would be a different life from mine, where I am active in the world. I think about people like Ramakrishna and Ramana and I can feel it, just being aware of yourself as pure consciousness, the absolute, and not as a functioning person. Maybe I'll drift into that in my old age. I'm having too much fun right now. You don't know what's going to happen next. That's what is so amazing. You can drop your whole life energy, your whole story, and just be.

Obviously time is something that is made up. It's a fabrication so that we can function. Everything's not happening at once. Time, personally for me, is pretty much non-existent. If it weren't for calendars and clocks I would be completely lost and even with them I'm pretty much lost. If I remember to look at them then I know what day it is and things like that. I live mostly outside of time except when I have to do something. They don't tell you that when you live in the now, in the present, you will not have a memory, but the good thing is that whatever you have to know will come to you, right in the nick of time.

For example, I might be sitting here, just relaxed, and then I look at my watch and it's ten o'clock, and I remember I have to pick up someone from town at ten o'clock. It wasn't there until that moment. There are so many things like that that I could tell you about. The anxiety around remembering things is not there. I don't carry a lot of information that I don't need. It's amazing. Especially when I was still nursing and I had lots of patients and had to remember everything, it felt very risky, but it is always there. It just functions on its own.

Basically, I don't think my personality has changed that much. My genes and my conditioning are still operating and I think those two things make the personality. My predilections are still the same. I have probably become more self-assured or confident. That comes from knowing who I am.

Certain tendencies have also remained. For example, when I was a kid, I remember that once we went to this farm and the guys were working out in the fields. We were sitting up on the porch, drinking iced tea. I went in to the fridge and got glasses of water and took them out to the guys in the field. Equality was always big with me. Wanting to help people who seemed to be not as well off.

All hospitals have used equipment that is still functional but just out of style. When I was in nursing school, they let me have it and I bundled it up and sent it off to people in Haiti and Mexico, and to Mother Theresa. That's something that has gone on throughout my life. It's not okay with me that children die every three seconds because they are too poor to stay alive while we are dying of obesity and diabetes. I like to even things out. That has remained and maybe become even more passionate, but there's less 'me' in it and it is less oriented towards results.

I remember politics in the sixties, marching on the Pentagon against the war in Vietnam, getting the Blacks registered to vote and all that. It was very different, very 'us and them', 'the good guys and the bad guys'. That's not there at all now. I just do it because I have to. I can't help it. It's like everything changes and everything stays the same. The form is the same but the energy is different. It's like the tree – it's the same tree but a different energy.

In this non-dual field it seems that there is sometimes the idea that there is nothing to do and you can get it in five minutes. I have known people who seem to get it very quickly. Sometimes this is just intellectual understanding and sometimes it's deeper but it's not solid. There's a lot of wavering and misunderstanding but they start teaching anyway. I feel that it would be better to sit with it for a while and let it become solid before hanging out the shingle. If they don't quite have it, then they are misleading or not saying it quite right to the people who come to them. There is more of that happening because of the nature of the non-dual teaching.

In the old days, when the masters got it, they left and went into a cave or a hut somewhere, away from the world, to sit with it until it became really solid or firm. People would go to them to ask questions and they would be told to go away. It was only when people would not go away that they gradually accepted one or two people to be around them. Now, that's an old model but that was my model.

I read somewhere that someone said, "My skin has become more of a thoroughfare than a barrier." I love that description because inner and outer can't be distinguished. It's the same as when you look at the tree. It's not separate. Inner and outer doesn't make sense as a concept.

there is no australia

I.D.A. What's happened to me? Gosh, that's assuming there is a me. We are starting with the assumption there is someone that this is happening to.

How I would have put it in the past? I'd say that I've been seeking a peace of mind for many, many years – maybe about thirty years. And while seeking, I've been through several different disciplines – religious ones, spiritual ones, Christian, Hindu, African, Shamanism, all sorts of different wonderful ideas, and I really enjoyed some of them, but they always came up with a list of how I should be, which did not resonate with me very well.

I've always had a stubborn streak in my nature. I just wasn't willing to go along with the idea that you are supposed to be this way in order to be 'enlightened' or 'find nirvana' or whatever you want to call it. I was brought up a Muslim. I gave that up in the mid seventies and I wasn't going to pick up another religion that told me how I am supposed to be. But that didn't stop me looking for something.

Some years ago, I think it was in the early nineties, I was in America at a men's retreat with Robert Bly and Michael Meade. We were all in the woods for about a week, there was a big lake and there was a sauna at the bank of the lake. I had an 'experience' there that really changed everything for me.

One night, a lot of men went to the sauna late at night. It was a mixed racial group. There were black men and white men and there was a Native American Indian chief. We were all sitting in the sauna, a bunch of maybe about thirty to forty men, and somebody suggested to the Native American: "Why don't you perform one of your ceremonies?" He agreed and he put his rug on the floor and took out his pipe and a few men made a circle around him. I was one of those who jumped at the opportunity to be sitting opposite him. He did a ceremony and we were all these naked men sitting there, smoking the pipe and calling the spirits to be present.

While the guy was doing the ceremony, something became important to me and I asked the question: "Just show me the way. Show me what is it. What is the truth? I want to know. How do I find this out? I have tried all sorts of things and nothing seems to gel, nothing seems to be the answer. Is there an answer?"

After it was over, we hung around outside and cooled down. It must have been about three or four in the morning. I chatted with all the other guys and then I decided to go back to the cabin. One of the guys who was sharing the cabin with me said: "I'm going back as well."

So we were both walking back to the cabin, two naked men walking out on this grassy slope of the lake on a moonlit night. Suddenly, I just stopped and he stopped and we just looked at each other and we just embraced. And all I can say is I disappeared. When I sort of came to, I said to him: "What happened?" He said: "I don't know. I just wasn't here." I said: "Me too. There was nothing, was there?" And he said: "No, there wasn't." Suddenly, there was a dawning. "Actually, everything is me – everything I'm seeing here – the dew – the grass!"

It's difficult to call it an 'experience', because it wasn't an 'experience'. It wasn't happening to me. So it wasn't thought-based experience. It was just something that happened that I couldn't understand. But it stayed with me.

I was studying psychotherapy at that time, doing my course at Regents College. I discussed this with my colleagues and the staff and they said: "This is what Freud called his 'oceanic experience'." I said: "No. I know what that is, but this wasn't an 'oceanic experience'. It wasn't that."

This wasn't an experience and of course how can you talk about not having an experience? And I couldn't answer the question. Except I knew that it wasn't anything that anybody else was saying. And then I spent the next maybe ten years trying to find out whether there was anybody who understood. I didn't understand it. And I was wondering if there was something wrong with me, actually? I kept looking and got involved in Shamanism and all sorts of different things.

❊   ❊   ❊

I went to one of the Ramana Maharshi satsangs here in London. It was fine but there was all the religious thing going on, where we sat down and candles were lit and people were chanting. I thought: "We're back into the same old game here," and I didn't want any of that.

Then I thought I'd better find out about this Tony Parsons guy that I'd heard about. When Tony started talking, within five minutes I thought to myself: "This guy can't say what he is saying unless he has a similar 'experience' like I did," and I immediately knew what he was saying.

I had questions. I was asking: "What about this and what about that", but slowly the questions dried up. It's like there aren't any questions to ask. You can't ask any questions because there is nothing to ask. Who is asking the question anyway? So if there is an individual here who is trying to understand something he's just going to ask the question. But there's no one here and there are no questions to ask anyway.

It changed my life. To say it changed my life is very strange, it's almost like saying I used to be different and now I am the same. It's like nothing's changed and yet everything has. It's difficult, because when you talk about this, then you're talking very much in terms of a person talking about it. It's almost a contradiction in terms. I still continue doing what I am doing, nothing's changed really in my life in that respect. But I suppose what has changed is that the anxiety has gone, the insecurity has gone. I don't worry about anything and I'm not concerned about anything. It's the realization that I'm just a character in a drama and things are happening constantly around me and I, as a character, will respond to those things in the manner that I would respond to them. And I don't actually have a choice in it. And it's fine. However it is is fine. It's got nothing to do with me anyway.

Is there a body here? Yes and no is the answer. There is a body and I've got to feed it. If I bang my head against the wall I'm going to feel pain, I'm going to feel hurt, so there is that physicality. It doesn't actually go away. But it's almost like it is not happening to someone. It's just what is happening in the appearance of things and this character acts and behaves in a particular way. But there is an awareness – more than awareness – it's kind of like: "It's happening, but it's not happening to me."

All of this is happening and all of this is me. There is only the one and it appears as if there is more than one. But there is just the one all the time. There is no separation.

I'm not sure if this is the right way to say it, but it's almost like it's happening in here *(touches chest)*. That fountain *(splashing outside)* is happening in here *(touches chest)*. Everything that is happening is being felt here, sensed here. So it's not outside of me, it's all here. And because it's here I am that here. Does that make sense? It's like if I wasn't here the fountain wasn't here. So whatever is present, the sounds and all of that, is happening here. That's all there is that's happening. But the minute I say it's happening in me, I'm talking about a body but that's not what I'm trying to say.

It's almost like you're just seeing it and it's amazing. Totally exquisite. Totally beautiful. It's just so fascinating, it's like: "Wow! Look at that!" Funny, you know, after a while it also becomes a very ordinary thing. It's like yeah, so what. Experience is thought based. Thinking causes experience. There is nothing actually happening but it is an appearance of something happening. There is no thing happening. It's an appearance. It appears to exist, it's not necessarily real. It's both real and unreal at the same time. In the drama there is an appearance of things, of manifestation, and that's what appears. But, in actuality, there is nothing there. So, in a sense, there's everything there and there is nothing there – at the same time.

The everything is an appearance in nothing. One isn't there before the other. It's just the appearance of nothing. Nothing appearing as something. You tend to see each person as an expression of nothingness. And there is no judgement. There is no "That's better and that's worse". It's just a different expression of the one.

❊　❊　❊

As a character, I have my preferences. I like to dress in a particular way, I prefer certain kinds of food, I like to live a certain kind of lifestyle. All sorts of things. I prefer a certain type of woman. I don't like this kind of man. All of that is there for this particular character. And that's fine. I can see that. There are some people I don't like. On another level, it's also like I'm not going to fight them or try and change them or make them be different because I can see that they are just another expression of the one. The one expression of a wino or a drug addict or a George Bush. I don't particularly like George Bush but that is a divine expression too, just as anything else. I don't like what he does, I have my feelings about that, but I'm not going to go up and try and fight it and try and change it because it's totally meaningless. It's just what happens. And from that perspective, it's also very exciting to see what happens, how it's going to turn out. I wonder what's going to happen next. Who knows?

The character lives in the world as safely as possible. I guess, in a sense, it's like being an animal. Animals aren't aware of dying and therefore they have no fear of dying, but they are also aware of danger and instinctively do things to avoid it. If I walk across the road and a bus arrives I'll instinctively jump out of the way. But I'm not preoccupied with what will happen if I die. All of those things about death and after-life, it's all just stories that people have made up to make themselves feel more comfortable. There is no heaven and there is no hell and there is no Father Christmas.

When I heard Tony Parsons speak, I instinctively knew what he was saying made absolute sense to me. There was no question about it. And I was blown away by it. It wasn't so much that it made sense in my mind, it's like I knew at some level, somehow I knew it already. It wasn't news to me and yet it wasn't ordinary. It wasn't something that everybody else was talking about or what I was brought up to believe or in all the seeking I'd done. This was it. This was what I knew and what I was holding onto – why I refused to fall in line with any other religious system or belief, however liberal or enlightened it might be – that I wasn't accepting – all the rules and regulations and things that you're supposed to do and not do. All that felt wrong to me.

What happened immediately after that was: "Yeah, but what about this and what about that?" Certain questions arose, mostly to do with my personal relationship with the woman I was living with at that time. In weeks it began to just resolve itself and immediately all of that came out. It was almost like: "This is it." And I don't care what else happens. It just makes absolutely no difference. I have no concern about how things are going to turn out because they will turn out the way they turn out.

We are just characters in a play. We're not the ones directing it. We look and we think as if we do but we don't. And in that respect there is a kind of place where it's exciting. What's going to happen next? How are things going to turn out? It doesn't mean that I don't do things that this character would do. If somebody needed some support or help or whatever it doesn't mean that I'm not going to provide that.

There's also something else. My brother phoned from South Africa. I was there in November with the family and he phoned me three weeks ago to tell me that his thirty-year-old son, who was a lawyer, had been murdered. Initially, I said: "What?" but afterwards – it sounds really callous – within minutes, it was like: "OK, so that's what happened." They are religious – Muslims – and I found it very interesting. He asked me: "How are you feeling about this? How is it for you?" And I said: "Well these things happen, you know." And my brother said: "From my perspective, it's God's rule. It was my son's time. His time came now and this is how he went," because my brother believes in Allah and that's what happens. So it's not dissimilar to the way I was looking at it, but it wasn't quite how I felt it. I was like: "These things happen." And they always happen. Sometimes they happen close to oneself and sometimes they happen not so close. It's just immaterial.

❋   ❋   ❋

When awakening happens, it doesn't happen to anyone. It's just what happens. You don't take it on. It's not something that is like: "Well I'll accept it" or "I'm going to live my life like this." That just doesn't happen. If it did, then it wouldn't work – it would be like a mental mind game that you're playing.

That's probably the biggest problem with the whole thing. People are trying to get somewhere where they can't get to. It's actually very, very obvious and a very simple thing really. It's just recognizing simply that there is nobody around. There's no one here, it's just the one splitting itself into different forms. And appearing in different forms. That's all it is.

You see the mind wants to experience that. And it cannot be experienced. That's the problem. You say to me that you understand on an intellectual level. Actually that's not the case. You understand because you know it. The mind wants to understand it and make it intellectual and rationalise it and say: "Oh, yes. I can see how that fits." But there is somewhere in you, you hear this and you're drawn to it. You know this. This is it. You know this already.

You already know this. You *already* know it. The mind comes and says: "Well I don't quite understand this." And *that's* the problem. The mind wants to understand something that you already know. And the mind can't understand it, because it's not logical. It's not rational. It doesn't make sense to the mind and the mind spends all its time trying to make sense of something it cannot make sense of.

But you see the wisdom, the truth in it. You know it. The mind says: "But I'm not feeling it." But a lot of times when you talk about feelings, they're not feelings at all. They're what I call 'felts'. Because they come from thoughts and thought is the past tense of thinking. And 'felt' is the past tense of feeling. So we are really 'thoughting' and 'felting' most of the time. And that's what the mind does. It's just 'thoughting' this, and then all these 'felts' come up. That's the way I think of it. The actual thinking and feeling has nothing whatsoever to do with this.

It's almost like a sensing. You know when you walk into a room and someone is having an argument and as soon as you walk in they stop arguing and you feel the atmosphere. You can sense it. You feel it. That's what I'm talking about. Sensing a feeling, if you just close your eyes and listen and hear all the sounds and noise and feel the sensations. This is what we're talking about. It's just feeling. Just sensing it. And you know this. You sense it.

You feel it and the mind comes in and says: "Yeah, but – " There is no "Yeah, but – " You *know*, but the mind says: "Yeah, but I don't quite get it" because the mind *can't* get it. It can never get it. The mind can never understand it. It's impossible.

✳ ✳ ✳

There are things that are enjoyed. I enjoy walking through woods in springtime and seeing things coming up and growing and there is enjoyment. I also enjoy other things that other people might not enjoy. But that's got absolutely nothing to do with it. That's just the character having this fun or that fun. But those moments of high anxiety or high elation don't exist.

I think all suffering happens fundamentally because people want things to be other than the way they actually are. That's all that suffering is about. People suffer because they want it differently. If people accepted things to be the way they are there is no suffering. Suffering happens in the drama, in the manifestation. Suffering happens. Pain happens. Joy happens. All of these things happen anyway. It's not happening to anybody, it's just what happens in the oneness. The oneness expressing itself in those ways.

Because I work as a psychotherapist, I've thought many times: "How do you get people to see this?" And, actually, you can't. I wondered whether you could make a film about it? I thought to myself: "Wouldn't that be boring." Because everybody would be OK about everything. There's no drama. There's no tension. There's nothing happening. It would almost be like zombies walking about, being OK about whatever is happening.

People whom I have spoken to about this tell me: "Yes, but I like the tension. I like the emotion. I like to feel the pain and the hurt when my woman fancies somebody else. I feel alive when I see a tragedy happen and I want to do something about it. It brings aliveness to me."

Yes, I can see that. Like when someone is going to watch Manchester United play football, they are really passionate about their team and there's this aliveness about it. People like that. They get something out of that. It gives a feeling of being part of something and really enjoying something. And a lot of people love it so much that they don't want it to be any different.

And then you tell them: "Well actually, you could be in a world where everything is more or less flat." And they say: "Well who wants it to be like that? What's the point of that? I want some passion in my life. I want to feel it. I want to feel loved. I want to feel sexually aroused, I don't just want to be flat." So I think to myself sometimes it could come across like being: "So what?"

A lot of people who are 'awakened' are people who have been seeking. Clearly whatever their life was like previously wasn't good enough for them. They were looking for something else. Mostly, I think it would be a peace of mind. They didn't want the drama in their life and the pulling of tensions from one extreme to the other – family squabbles – relationship problems – work problems – problems with other people. Racism and sexism. All of that.

These people are looking for something else. They go out seeking and they tend to look for a spiritual power where everything is beautiful and nice and lovely and beautiful flowers and doves flying through the sky and peace and everyone is loving to each other. After a while, they find out that this is nonsense. This is not true. So they keep seeking. And ultimately I think that one tends to see that all of it is OK. You are all of it. Then what happens is the person, the individual, stops existing. You are no longer there. And when you are no longer there, then everything is seen for what it is.

I remember being in the States some years ago. One of the big television broadcasters – NBC or CNN – had advertising billboards and the slogan was: "Satisfies your need to know". I thought that was so beautiful. Yes, it got you by the jugular because that's what everyone wants. They want to know.

Where there is nothing to know, absolutely nothing to know, there is nothing. And that's the beauty of it. And our stories, our life stories that go on in psychotherapy – this story and that happened – it's rubbish. It's total nonsense. It's just the mind making up this whole idea: "This means this and that means that", and giving this significance, giving reasons for why this happened. We haven't got a clue why anything happens. We think this happened because of that, but that's just what we made up.

In actuality, there is no meaning to anything. Life is totally meaningless. There is no purpose. We are not going anywhere. There is nothing happening. There is nowhere to go to. There is nothing to do. And 'doing' happens and "going" happens and all of that happens – but it actually has no purpose to it. There is no meaning to anything. It is totally meaningless. But the mind gives things meaning because it feels comfortable giving meaning. It feels comfortable knowing things. If it can understand things or make sense or give something meaning, this is how it feels comfortable.

Why did the Berlin Wall come down when it came down? It came down when it came down because that's when it came down! Who the hell knows why it came down? Yet we write a whole lot of reasons as to why it came down – well, it's totally meaningless. Why did apartheid end when it ended and not before or later? It just so happened right then. That's all. Things just happen. But the mind wants to make some sense of it, give some meaning to it. We do that with our own life stories. All the drama, our lives, so meaningful. I think Shakespeare put it very well many years ago when he said: "A story told by an idiot full of sound and fury, signifying nothing." Totally meaningless. But some people like the drama.

From a psychotherapy perspective, we notice that suffering comes from people wanting things to be other than they actually are. That's simply an observation. But in terms of seeing from 'oneness', it's just simply things happening. And it doesn't have a purpose to it or a meaning to it. When you see that, there is this place of letting things be, however they are.

Is there a feeling of detachment? In some ways yes, in other ways no. You're fully alive and you feel fully connected and at the same time you're not pulled in and drawn into it. You're engaged in life. I've got work to do and I have management meetings and all that kind of stuff. You've got all these things that you're doing as a character. The character plays all that, except the intensity goes away, but you're not sitting back and letting it all happen. You're totally engaged, but you're engaged in a way where there's no emotional investment in the outcome. Because it's not in my power to know that. It may go that way, then it may not. However it turns out, it is OK.

It's very ordinary actually. It's really very ordinary. There's nothing more. I'm not suddenly the bookcase. The bookcase isn't me. There's none of that spiritual stuff. It's very ordinary. It's simply, if you like, whatever appears in my awareness now is all there is. That's all there is. There is nothing else.

There is no Australia. There is no Australia other than an idea in our heads. All you've got now is an idea in your head that there is somewhere called Australia. That's all there is. Where is Australia? Show me. So all there is right now is an idea in your head that there's Australia. That's all there is. The foyer downstairs. It doesn't exist. It just arises in your awareness. So when we walk out, it's just what appears – constantly appears for us. It's creating the space as it expands. It's not expanding into space.

I think it was Emmanuel Kant the philosopher who said: "The world appears not the way it is but the way you are". Because we can never ever actually see it as it is. We can only see it as we see it. It's like an appearance.

It's not so much to do with you. It's simply what is happening. It's not personal. None of this is personal.

There is no one to whom this is happening. We tend to see it always from a personal perspective. "This is happening to me." When, simply, what is happening is not at all personal. But our minds always get in there and say: "Oh, see, this happened and that happened too."

I have some private clients and three of them had to pay me last week. The first said: "I've forgotten my cheque book. I'll send you a cheque." And I said "OK." The next one that I saw said: "Actually, I only bought enough money for this session but I'll put a cheque in the post" and I said: "OK." The third said exactly the same: "I haven't got my chequebook here. Can I post you a cheque?" And I said: "Fine." And I told my partner: "Isn't that interesting. They don't know each other and yet all my clients have managed somehow not to pay me this week. And they all said they are going to post it and none of them have posted it. Isn't that interesting?" I could then look into myself and say: "What did I do? Why is this happening to me?" All that kind of rubbish. Or else I can see it as I do see it. It is very simply: "That's what's happening. That's simply what happened."

All kinds of things happen and our minds tend to make sense of it. That's what the mind does. It makes sense and gives reasons and causes and why's and because's and all of that. That's what the mind does. We haven't got a clue. It's simply things happening. Simply. My mind can come in there and say: "This must mean this and that must mean that" and so on. It's very easily done. Very, very easily done.

This is what the mind does. It's always trying to understand, trying to know, trying to figure it out. All of that. Trying to survive. And all it's trying to do is survive itself. All the mind is doing is trying to protect itself. As if it is insecure and as if it is the one that's in control, *when it isn't.*

That's the message really. That we are not in control. We assume we are. We make choices. We make decisions. Or so it appears. All of it is simply an appearance. It's about waking up from the dream. Into the dream.

total freedom and total anarchy

Y. S. I'm a female, I'm forty-nine years old and I'm an artist. I live in Amsterdam.

About one and a half years ago, the 'seeing' happened, if that's the way to say it. I had been searching, searching, meditating, doing groups, listening to Osho, all these things that everybody did.

And one day, I had been at dinner with some very good friends of mine. We had talked about how I had been living in a commune for a couple of years and the slogan was: "Make things better in the world. Make better people." That was the attempt of the community. We had been talking about how ridiculous that is – to want to 'make people better'. And yet, that is exactly what we had been trying all the time.

And then, on my bike going home, it suddenly hit me – really, really hit me – that all my attempts to be a 'better person' were absolutely ridiculous. That was one thing.

Then the next day, I drove to Luxembourg, where I've been doing a lot of business. I was in the car on the road in Belgium, driving fast, and I suddenly started to cry and scream. I was so angry because of all my attempts my whole life to be a better person seemed so trivial. Everything that had happened in my life. I was really angry and shouting.

And then suddenly, the veil lifted. Suddenly within all that turmoil it was as if a veil just fell on the floor or whatever. It lifted and I looked into this. God, I just still get ... I looked into this and there was no future, no past, nothing had ever happened. Oh God ... it's still amazing.

It's like ... it was incredible. And at the same time, I was driving my car. I was seeing that there was no past, there never had been a past and also I had always known this. This had always been like this. There was no history. There was no attempt. There was nothing. There was absolutely nothing. It was amazing.

And at that moment, the weird thing wasn't even that I felt grateful. I felt pissed off. Because of the joke that had been played on me. My whole life I tried so hard – like we all do – and struggled and suddenly, there was nothing to do. There was nothing to see. There it was. Just this. This is all there is. So that's how it happened. It didn't happen, but 'seeing' happened. There was no doing – no me – just, it was seen.

And then everything kept going. I mean life just happened after that. It was just two days before a retreat with Tony Parsons. I went to the retreat but I didn't really want to go. It had been pretty amazing what had happened and at the same time nothing had happened – so you just go about your business of driving in your car, talking to people and all this. And at the same time, there was seeing.

I went to the meeting with Tony. The first evening, it was very strange. I was looking at him – he was speaking in the group – it was as if the words that came out of him, came out of me. There was no boundary, nothing. It sounds like something special or esoteric. It wasn't. It was just there was no more boundary at all.

It was as if I was speaking the words. It wasn't that I was him – not in that way. It was more that the words that he said were my words. It was as if the words that he said were coming out of me. I can't explain it. And it was nothing esoteric. It was just wonderful. At some point, a woman that I have seen in the seminars already for so many years – she got up and asked the same question that she had already asked in all the meetings – and suddenly I could see that the only thing between her and 'seeing' was the thought that she was a person. That was all. It was so thin and I wanted to get up and shout at her: "You idiot! Wake up!" It's just so thin, so easy. And she's there – she sees it – it is just this veil, that's all. It was very amazing. Yeah.

It's very hard putting words to it. It would seem like something esoteric or something weird, which it wasn't. No thought was there. There was no thought. There was just the words arising, jumping up or coming out. Exactly in the right place, as they should be. Something like that.

When all this started to be seen, everything seemed very ambiguous. What bugged me the first couple of months was that everything seemed so 'both this and that'. It seemed very natural and at the same time it was amazing. I felt in awe and at the same time it was very natural. There is this wonderful, wonderful, wonderful, wonderful beauty. At the same time, it's just so simple and so natural and emotionless.

✳   ✳   ✳

I started to do meditation about the end of my twenties. Because I was unhappy, I was looking for a way to get more happy – to lead a fulfilling life. So I went to Osho. I was a sanyassin for a couple of years, I did many meditation groups and I lived in a community, 'working with people for a better world'. When Osho died, I stopped being a sanyassin. I dropped the name and all that and I became interested in Barry Long, which lasted a couple of years.

At some point, I was fed up with all teachers. I went to live in Aruba, where I was born. It's a small island in the Caribbean. It used to be Dutch. I lived there for two years and I was absolutely, wonderfully happy because I had no parents around, no friends telling me what to do, nothing. It was the first time I was just me. Actually, it was a feeling of coming home, which I hadn't had before. I made many so-called mistakes and I had a wonderful time of being, partying, without anybody interfering. Without anybody's judgement or whatever.

Anyway, I came back and I was introduced to Tony Parsons, which was probably three years ago. Mostly I went because friends of mine were very enthusiastic. In the beginning, I didn't really want to be there and I thought: "God. Another teacher." But he is so sweet and so normal and ordinary. I started to help out at meetings.

And maybe the second or third time I was there, I was so angry and I remember getting up at one point and I said: "I want this! I want you to give it to me!" I was very angry that what he said seemed so simple and I didn't get it. I got really angry and pissed off. I wanted it at that moment. And it didn't happen then. When I stopped looking, and I didn't stop looking consciously, that was it.

When 'seeing' happened, it found me. It found me. There was no doing, there was no wish in that moment when it happened. It just found me. It's amazing. You can't make a conscious decision to stop looking. So really in that moment when I was very, very desperate, I felt really *really* desperate in everything. My love life was always fucked up with men and I was trying to be a different person, to be a better person. And, when I gave that up, I got the visit. It's not like that, but suddenly it found me.

When that happened in the car, I saw that it had nothing to do with anything that I had done before, like meditations. All my searching has been in vain. All my searching, all the grouping, all the talking, all the writing, it has been in vain because you cannot want it consciously or demand it. It doesn't work that way. But it's here.

For me, it is there all the time but the movie goes on. So I may still get emotional about some things, even though I notice that it is different now. It is like you welcome everything. Everything is absolutely perfect for me, whatever happens. Come! That could be anger, that can be everything.

✳ ✳ ✳

The first few months so many miracles happened. There were so many new ways of seeing – or sudden seeing. All my beliefs were shattered. The first few months, it was very explosive 'seeing'. Pieces of puzzles falling in the right place.

I remember that I was waiting for the tram and I was looking at people and suddenly seeing that there was nobody there. It was just a body. That's the way it is. Puzzle pieces falling in place.

Just a couple of weeks ago, I was sitting in the tram and two people came in. They were drunkards or junkies and my mind started, the machinery started with the judgements: "It's not a good life". And suddenly, it dropped away. I could see that the 'quality of life' was intact in them. Life didn't care if these people were drunks. The so-called 'quality' was exactly the same in them as in me or in the tram. In anything. In the cars. It's life. It doesn't have a judgement about whether these people are drunks.

I could see that it is just the mind which likes to throw things on people. The judgement machinery goes on and on, but it seems to drop away more easily or quicker. It's not something that *I* do. So, if the machinery starts with the judgement, it's fine by me. It doesn't bother me. It's fantastic if all judgement drops away. But also if judgement is there, it's fine too, you know? It doesn't matter in the whole story.

❈   ❈   ❈

It was wonderful. Things happened a lot in the beginning, frequently, like looking at myself, falling in love with this *(points to herself)*. That was a big thing, a wonderful thing. Falling in love with this. Welcoming everything that happens, everything. Falling in love with everything that I am.

Before, when doing therapy, I think my whole life I've tried to *be* somebody, to please people. Pleasing people in jobs, in everything, with friends, everybody. And that's what is dissolving or dissipating. I don't have to please anybody anymore. And that is possible, if you start to welcome everything that arises in you. So it may be anger, it doesn't matter, it is something that just comes and goes and it's of no importance really.

But the basic thing is that all of it is welcomed. And it's none of my doing. I am not doing it. I am not consciously welcoming whatever arises. It's impossible. It's not a conscious choice for any of that. It's falling in love with everything – with everything that arises. All the beautiful stories in the world, whatever the story is – or my own story or your story or the story of the floor – it's all wonderful. It's hard to describe.

And it's nothing holy. That was one of the things that bugged me and bugs me still. None of the things I thought that *this* was, it is. All the books I read. My God! All the discussions we had about it or listening to the masters. It is none of that. It is so incredibly obvious and simple. Nothing changes and everything changes.

❊   ❊   ❊

The first few months were filled with paradoxes. But this is the first time I have talked about it like I'm talking to you now. I don't talk about it with friends. I don't talk to anybody about it. I find that very hard because of the words, because of the fear of distorting it. It is hard for me to talk about it because sometimes there is the thought: "It can't be this simple."

That is the in and out movement as well. There can be doubt. Anything can arise. That's just it. Anything can arise and beneath that is the knowing. The simplicity of this. Just accept everything that arises, just love everything that arises.

You can't grasp it. You cannot understand it. It will find you. You can't get it and it is so simple. If you look at the meetings with teachers, all these people come like I did, every year, every time, asking the same questions. Not stupid questions, but just not this. Questions that don't matter. There is a wish – of course you would want everybody to see it, because that would be great. Yeah.

❊ ❊ ❊

Whenever you start to say: "Oh, maybe I'm just thinking it" – it's a thought. You are starting to label it like we're all crazy about doing. We love labelling and putting it in a meaningful box.

That is one of the wonderful things about this. The giving up. When you give up wanting or desiring to change what is. But then again you cannot want or desire that.

You can't make that happen. Therefore, it is maybe sad that we all have to search and read in a way. I feel a sadness now that I wish you would see it too.

The world doesn't make sense at all to me. It doesn't have to. It's senseless. To me it seems that there is no sense exactly. There is no purpose. It is absolutely just enjoyment. No, even that is not true. It is just what is, which could be enjoyment, which could be fear, which could be anger, which could be anything.

❋ ❋ ❋

A word which is much used, which I used to hear a lot, is 'attachment'. I feel less 'attached' to any of the emotions that pass through, could pass through. Maybe fear would come up and it would attach to this person and I would be: "Oh God, I'm so fearful." And now it's not a conscious thing, but fear may come up and it is just fine. And even if it's not fine, and if I hate it and think I don't want this fear, that's fine too. Anything can come up. There's no more fighting this. There's no fighting anything. And if there is fighting? That's fine. Even the fighting or the resisting of the emotion is OK with me.

Before, I used to think I was not allowed to judge because I wanted to be a holy person and I thought it didn't fit with being a seeker to judge – and of course I did judge all the time. And now I see it differently. Judging doesn't mean anything. I don't have a problem with judging anymore. And if I have a problem with judging then I have a problem with judging. So that's fine too. Judgements are nothing different than any emotion or anything that arises. Judgements are great, wonderful, just get them out. It doesn't matter. I am judging. There is no doubt about it, I do judge but I don't care about it. And if I care – I may feel bad about it sometimes – then I feel bad about it. It's the same thing as before with the anger.

❋ ❋ ❋

I have been very busy with trying to make a living this

last year, so this is not really very good for creativity. Before, when I was really into emotions, all these things *(points to art works)* are very emotional, they represented emotions. That somehow has changed. I don't know what will happen but it is different. I haven't made any art really, it is much cooler. I don't know what it will bring but it did change. Actually I was more artistic before than now. But again it doesn't matter to me because I will see what happens and how it will evolve. But it *is* different.

This is something *(points to piece of art)* which is just a beginning but it's much more quiet and still and so in that way it's different. I don't have outbursts of emotions anymore really. I don't know how that works. I think that is because of the attachment. If you welcome anything it can come and go easily and quickly. And it affects making of art. We'll see what happens. I'm curious. I'm really looking forward every day to what this day is going to bring. And that could be boredom as well. That's another thing that fell away. I don't have an expectation about anything anymore. I don't expect the day to be grand or wonderful. I don't expect that I will make a masterpiece today. I don't expect anything.

✳ ✳ ✳

I don't speak about it, so at this moment it is still implementing in my life and being in the wonder of it often and just enjoying that for me. It's not that I don't want to speak about it, but I also noticed that people love the drama. We all love our drama so what I can say could be very cold sometimes or cutting it off. So that stops me often. I just noticed that sometimes you *do* want to shout it out.

This is what worries me often – if you start putting words to things. Sort of fear of interfering with anybody's life, their perception or whatever. I would just prefer to leave everything to everybody the way it is. We are totally free creatures and I think that's the beauty. To me this is total freedom and total anarchy as well. I am not part of a group. I just live as I live – my ordinary life and that's just what I do. Religion has nothing to do with this. That is what started to be seen when I started to 'see'. All my notions about everything were misconceptions – about religion, about how I should live, how you should live. The world is misconception.

If I had to put words to it, it is total freedom. Total freedom to let anything arise that arises. It is total freedom to be whoever you are and embrace the character that you are. It is total anarchy. It is total freedom and total anarchy.

Within that life, if rules need to be followed, go ahead and follow the rules. This is the very tricky part. People in meetings always ask: "Yes, but what if I would kill somebody?" If one could grasp it, if you could really see that this is just a big, big game in which everything can happen or can arise. I think this is something that people don't really want to hear. Fear that one might start killing people is a question that arises out of attachment. It's all mind. It's all bullshit.

At the same time apparently, looking at the news, people kill each other. This is what happens and, in my understanding, it will always be like this. There is no better world we will ever get. I used to think that the goal was to get everybody enlightened. Well, it isn't. There is no goal. There is no purpose.

❊ ❊ ❊

I'm not saying, by the way, that I might not cry if my cat dies. Of course, in this body, there is still attachment. The fear has to do with attachment to bodies. It's very hard. It's difficult because it's totally out of the understanding system of our world. In this world, we are so much attached to all our things, our people, our friends, our family, and that has nothing to do with this. With living in this.

It is like a mystery every day. The character stays the character, but the character cannot be described, either. You can't say: "Oh, this person will never do this or that," and that is just a joy. That is absolutely wonderful. The freedom is every day: "Let the character be. Evolve. Be." And that's freedom.

That is another thing which is hard to tell people: "There is only life. There is no death." The body may drop away, but life is all there is. Life is in everything. That's why grief is ridiculous. It's attachment again. You attach life to this particular body and that's it. But life is all the time present, it's in everything. It is all there is. You're not going anywhere. When I die or when the body drops away, that's all that happens. The body drops away. And it doesn't matter. It is an ongoing play of life. Life is continuously throwing up games for people to play. Throwing up people, throwing up nice ideas and wonderful things, that's all. And it will always be like that.

In your life you have certain parts in your life which you think keep you going or whatever. It's attachment. There is only, only, only life. There is nothing else. And all *this* is the manifestation of this life. Everything, everybody.

I remember another thing that happened. In the first few months I saw *everything* reflect this too. It is like shouting out to us all the time. It can be a word, it can be a song. It is all shouting out. We're sitting here now. Everything here is shouting out at you and me: "This is it!" I cannot explain it differently. All the time, everything in your life which arises is a manifestation of this. It is continuously trying to grab your attention, not as if it had a purpose, but that's what it is doing. If you walk outside, even the street is shouting at me. It is wonderful.

❊ ❊ ❊

I don't have any light flashes or things like that. I don't have any of those kind of things. It's not happening for this person anyway. That is the paradox. It is so down to earth, and at the same time, whenever I try to put a word to it, it sounds something like energy.

When I was with Osho, he was a beautiful person, but very distant. I thought I had to become this person, a kind of holy man, and I thought that this was 'enlightenment'. Tony Parsons made it so simple and down to earth, which possibly helped me to recognise the moment. And to be able to cope with it.

When it happened, for a couple of months I was sort of fearful that I might get crazy as well at times, but it didn't happen. It is a big thing to incorporate in the body. Also a paradox at the same time. It is completely obvious and nothing special. Completely simple because it is so not of the world, none of our opinions or conceptions.

Another description might be: it was a sort of complete relaxation, a complete relaxation into whatever would arise. And that's basic. Relaxation in whatever arises. Welcome it, love it, but without doing it.

being the sea

C.T. I'm fifty-eight-years old. I graduated from Melbourne University with an Honours Degree in Economics. I'm a strategic consultant. I'm a business person. I've been doing that for nearly twenty-five years. Before that I spent years in industry, managing companies, and in corporate finance. So most of my life I've been in business. I've been married for most of my life – married for thirty-five years to the same woman, and I've got four beautiful grownup children. I have a very complex rich and diverse life and I'm involved in many, many things.

The thing that you want to talk about and the thing that I'm quite happy to talk about has got nothing to do with any of that. It's sort of a different thing altogether.

✳   ✳   ✳

I started off in my twenties becoming a seeker – the classic spiritual seeker – starting off with Alan Watts. I think *The Supreme Identity* was the first thing I read. Then on and on to Taoism and Buddhism and Sufism and every 'ism' you could think of. I was into

61

it for a good ten years or so. There's a value in that stuff – no doubt about it. There's a value in what I call the 'spiritual pornography', because that's what it is – porn. At that stage in your development you need it. It supports you. It gives you some insights. It's the mind trying to take itself to the edge of its own limitations.

Even though I'm very familiar with most of the religious traditions, I would certainly not classify myself as religious. In fact, religion is an anathema to me. I think what Jung said about religion is essentially right. Jung said: "Religion is a defence against the experience of God" and that is pretty much it in a nutshell. At the same time, the mystical traditions have a great deal to teach us. That's why I love them, but they don't form a major part of my life in terms of ritual nor do I sit on my bum for eight hours a day. I have practised yoga a lot over the years. It's been very valuable to me at a particular stage in my life but I don't regularly sit now. I am very fit physically. I think physical fitness is very important.

❉   ❉   ❉

You arrive at a point where you just can't go much further with the mental models and you start letting go of it. Something very strange happens. I suppose the Christians would call it 'grace', where, in the letting go, in stopping the seeking, all of a sudden there is a realization – it's almost like the dissolving of the personality.

For me, it didn't happen all at once. All of a sudden, I would get insights. Then I would be back with C.

again, identified with C. and in and out of that state. And that still happens to me. I still spend times when I'm very identified with C. I have to remind myself to go back to being who I really am. I don't think it is so easy to completely escape from your personality. The conditioning is very strong.

One of the things that's always interested me is: "Why is it that our natural tendency is to be contracted and identified with the born being – instead of being identified with that other consciousness? Why is it so?" I don't know the answer, other than it just seems to be the way it is. Our tendency is to default to familiarity.

Most people identify with the personality that they've inherited or acquired over their life. So if you were Jane, you identify with Jane, you think you are Jane, you think you are all of the things that Jane is. She really is a personality. She has likes, she has dislikes, she has moods, she gets sick, she's happy some days, she's sad other days. Good things happen to her, bad things happen to her, and one day some terrible thing's going to happen to her. She's going to die, which is not great for Jane. In Jane's life there is a lot of fear because she's identified with the 'born being'.

I think, for me, realisation has been an awareness: I am not *that* one who is going to die. So it genuinely is a matter of what do you identify with. It's such a simple thing in a way. It's such a simple thing.

And when you see it, it's so obvious and you think: "My goodness me! Why didn't I see that before? How come I've been identified with that poor little chap all this time, struggling away being him?" It's not that you cease being him. That doesn't happen. I mean C. is still here. C. is very active in the world. He's a father, he's a lover, he's a business person. He provides advice to not-for-profit organisations. He does good works. He does silly things. He enjoys himself. He eats too much. He drinks too much sometimes – all those things. It's not that he disappears. It's just that I understand that there is much more to C. than meets the eye.

I don't really talk about it very much. I have no need to talk about it. If I do talk about it, and sometimes people are interested to talk about it, there are many different metaphors that you can use to describe this. It's a bit like a closed fist. You can identify with that sort of contracted state, which is the self, or you can just open your hand, let go of it.

Or imagine that you're a fish swimming in the ocean. You're a beautiful silver fish and you're swimming along in this watery ether. You have eyes, gills, fins, you're breathing in the water. You are the fish. Now just imagine for a minute that you're *not* the fish, that you're actually the ocean in which the fish is swimming. Imagine that you're that ether which is giving rise to everything that happens in it.

The ocean treats all of the inhabitants of the ocean equally. It doesn't discriminate between sharks and jellyfish and octopi – the good guys and the bad guys. It supports all of them equally. The ocean makes no distinction. It doesn't judge, pass judgements about all the creatures that live there. It supports all of them equally. Jellyfish are as supported by it as sharks or snappers or any other form of life in the ocean.

It's nothing actually and yet it's everything. So, it just is. It's the 'is'. That's one way of talking about it. Be the sea and not the fish. Be the 'Sea of Being'.

What happens when you become the sea? Everything and nothing. Your life changes and it doesn't. In one sense it changes dramatically because the whole standpoint of your existence changes. You lose your fear. You are no longer concerned about your appearance in the world. I'm not worried about C. anymore. He's just doing what he does and he's fine. So that's a wonderful thing.

At the level of C., he still operates. I think he operates a lot better. There are some very good benefits. I've found this as I've brought this state of being into my work – I do a lot of workshops, facilitation, strategy planning exercises – and when you are operating from this standpoint, somehow people just know. They just know something is different and they resonate very strongly with it. Somehow, things just work. I often go into meetings not terribly well prepared. I don't worry about that anymore because I just trust in who I am.

I say to people, if you could only – it makes me laugh – it's like flicking a light switch. It's just a little tiny step. It's like Alice going through the looking glass. Walking through the mirror.

Douglas Harding's got an exercise – it's good fun actually and very valuable – he gives people a little piece of white cardboard with a hole cut in it about the size of their face. There's a little piece of mirror also glued to the cardboard. Initially, he gets them to look in the mirror so they're looking at this face which they identify with. Then he says: "Now I want you to put on immortality." He gets them to stand back and slowly bring this piece of cardboard right up to their face and put it on. They go through and think: "Oh, my God. There's nothing here!" There's nothing – but everything. He says: "You become the space for things to happen in." You become the sea and not the fish. The sea that is available for everything. The sea that is open to everything. The sea that is not needy. There is nothing there to need anything.

Strange business. So is it delusion? If it is, I prefer to be deluded. If a psychologist was sitting here, they might say: "This chap's got some sort of psychosis. He's schizophrenic. He doesn't think he's C." They would have some conventional psychological explanation and say: "It's not real."

You only have to experience this condition and the joy of it and the bliss that goes with it to realise that it's totally real. So many of the problems in the world today arise simply because we are so conflicted, we're so identified with our personalities, our face, we're so aggressively defensive of that, at the individual level or at the state level or at the tribal level. All of that stuff goes away when you stop identifying with that person.

Most of modern civilisation actually reinforces us to go back into the mind – to live in the mind. Even the religious traditions are essentially mental, egoically-based activities. They've got nothing to do with spiritual realization – nothing at all. That's not to say they're bad either.

❊   ❊   ❊

One of the things about this realisation, if you want to call it that, is that you don't say "no" to things anymore. I don't think you're actually there until you pretty much say "yes" to everything. The sea doesn't say "no" to things. All the things that swim in it, it says "yes" to them. It supports them all.

George Bush, horrible though he may be, he's part of it. He's one of the fish, as were the chaps who flew the planes into the World Trade Center. It's not a matter of taking sides. These days I'm more concerned – not about what I'm for or against – but with the need to be in charge of it. When I do form judgements about things, as far as possible, they're grounded in (or they come out of) my higher state, if you like.

Although the higher self doesn't form judgements or make choices, somehow or other C. does have to operate in the world and he does have to make choices. That's the nature of being human. You have to make choices. What I have found increasingly over the years is that the choices I make are made more slowly. They come almost out of a process. They arrive. The choices emerge. I let the process work.

There's such a massive emphasis these days on productivity. We identify the results of our labours: "He's a wealthy man." "He's got a five hundred foot cruiser." "That guy's got a red sports car." We identify with productivity. I think it's essentially fear based. They're not the sort of choices that come out of a more holistic understanding of who you are.

An apricot tree doesn't produce apricots. It *bears* them. Fruits are gifts. I think, in my own case, what happens increasingly is you allow, you recognise, you understand that a large part of the way in which you work in the world has to do with what you are – as opposed to what you're trying to make or produce. And you have to trust that. There's an element of faith in it as well. A Christian would call that faith. Trusting that your inherent goodness will produce good choices, letting it help you make good choices. And it does. It's amazing. I don't do much anymore at all, sort of consulting by turning up, you know? In the Tao they talk about Wu Wei – work without effort – and I think that's actually what it means. It means you don't really have to struggle too much or try too hard. You just have to trust.

Life is living us – but we are still there. I think it's wrong to deny the fact that there is an individuated energy there.

There is only one identity. There's only one reality. Everything's arising in it. There's only one consciousness. In some of my environmental talks I say to people: "You think that you're in some way independent of the natural world? Well, fine, I'd like you to stop breathing for five minutes, if you don't mind." It makes the simple point that we're so much part of nature.

I think that's the truth of things. There is only one of us here and it's not a one which you can really talk about. Stuff is arising the whole time and yet I still live in a world where there is a C. and he makes choices and those choices have consequences. So who is making the decisions? That's where the two things are completely running together. It's very important not to deny the existence of the 'born being'. I don't deny him. Nor do I identify with him. See people want either/or – but it's both.

Even at a scientific level, we know that if you take this table, and you go in close enough, it disappears. It just becomes vast amounts of space. It's not what we think it is. None of it is. So it's truly awesome. The creation is truly awesome and wonderful.

One of the other things that for me has been wonderful is this realisation all the time that it didn't have to happen. The miracle is that I'm here, that my consciousness is present to talk to you. That's just miraculous. How'd it happen? That wonderful sense of "Wow!" all the time. The miracle of existence all the time – in the small things, in small creatures, in plants, in form, in built structures, gives you a completely different sense of aesthetic beauty. There's not a thing in my life that I don't view as a friend – things that I build, chairs that I like, they're just amazing appearances that are part of my life. I'm a furniture maker in my spare time. You make something and you look at it, and think: "Hello! Welcome! Look at you! Aren't you gorgeous? Where'd you come from?" A re-arrangement of the atoms. It's just magical in the extreme. Just wonderful.

I don't think I'm a fully realised adept or anything like that. I don't know what they are. I'm not interested either. I just live my life. Earlier on, when I was younger, I had some drug-induced experiences which were pretty good, you know? You walk through the mirror – through the looking glass – and in some of those states you do realise absolutely there's only one consciousness. It's all alive. That's it. So I had those experiences when I was younger, loved it. I also had some pretty bad experiences which pretty much put me off that path for all time.

On a number of occasions in different places at different times, when I was probably in my forties, I had insights which were really profound, where you just *know*. You just see it fully.

It took a long time for me to – I wouldn't say arrive at the same place – because it was different. It was more gentle. It was less immediate. It was more natural.

Once, in an aeroplane flying from Melbourne to Sydney, all of a sudden, *"Boom!"*, I've just gone – *disappeared*. I'm in the aircraft, there's just nobody there and there's just all these wonderful creatures sitting there and all the furniture. The chairs were beautiful. I loved every one of them, you know? All of the lovely fittings. It was just miraculous. Nobody there at all. So you sit there for an hour in that state and you get off and you're still in that state and the rest of the day you're still in that state. Slowly, when you go home to the kids and your wife, you sort of get drawn back into conversation. You tend to go back to being C. again. That happened a lot.

Douglas Harding's little experiments are quite helpful, every now and again, in reminding yourself of who you are. I went through a period where I found those experiments quite helpful in bringing you back to the understanding of who you really, really are.

In the last seven or eight years, I've just let go. I'm just trusting more in life. Fear is largely gone. That is the key to it. I just know now who I am and I trust it and I can rely on it. It is one hundred per cent bankable. And there's wonderful joy, tremendous love. That's what it is, you know? So you just come to rely on that, *be* that. Why would you want to be anything else?

No one's perfect here. I sometimes get jolted back into that other state by something happening. A couple of years ago, my son was in a very bad car accident. We got the news at midnight. The police rang. And that really jolted me. Just for a time there I was back being the father and terribly upset and concerned about the fact that he might be critically injured. He was badly injured but he was okay, as it turned out. All of a sudden – the fear, the identification with the 'born being', the anxiety about what might happen – all those things back again.

That is when you need to practise the conscious process. You must make it a conscious process to go back to the centre and go back to being who you know you really are. And just allow and allow and allow. When I went into the casualty area where they were working on him, he was covered in blood and they were stitching him up. It was pretty terrible. But he was conscious. I suddenly saw then I was back and could see the whole thing working. It was just a wonderful orchestra of stuff happening to heal him, fix him up and I didn't have to be concerned. You shift back and you think: "Everything's fine."

Even when worse things happen. My nephew – twenty years old – was killed in a hit and run accident. I'll never forget my wife running across the ground at the farm to tell me that he had been killed. And that was interesting because it did not throw me out. It always felt OK. That sounds really weird but it always felt OK he had been killed. I know his parents – my sister – suffered terribly and still are, but I've always known that it was fine and he's fine.

❊ ❊ ❊

I've never had the blue lights and the trumpets and the visitations of the shaking shakti or whatever. That hasn't been my journey. It's been much more gentle. You read stories about people 'waking up' through koans or zen meditation and suddenly they're permanently established. That hasn't been my experience.

I think I was too mental for that. I'm a very mental person. I'm a very, very bright guy with an incredibly powerful mind, which I worked on for years. I made it. It was a deliberate effort to turn it into a weapon. It's pretty hard to deal with once you've got it. It wants to run the show all the time. It's super powerful, and having constructed the 'death star' – the *Star Wars* metaphor – you can't deconstruct it that quickly. You've got to wear it out a bit. That was one reason why it was a slower process, more of a dissolving rather than being able to leave it behind like that.

The mind's very helpful. The mind's a good thing in its place. Being identified with the mind is horrible. It's a state of imprisonment. It's just terrible. It's hell. So learning that you are not your mind, that the mind is just one part of reality ... there's so much more to it.

It's not my thoughts. It's not my body. No. It's not either of those. It's not feeling. It's not any of those things. It's just *is*. *Is* is.

'Is' is alive. 'Is' is aware. 'Is' is conscious, pure consciousness, pure awareness. The sea is alive. It's aware. Douglas Harding used to talk about an 'ether', you know, the glassy ether, or the glassy essence. It's just aware presence.

One good way of describing it is all that stuff that is happening is on a screen. It's all playing on a screen – but the screen is not the images that are projected onto it. The screen's nothing. It's nothing.

I pretty much know who I am and I am very aware of what thoughts are going on. Thinking is happening, good quality thinking is happening, ordered thinking is happening a fair bit of the time – but it's happening in a context of nothing, just this being.

The awareness is not thinking. It's not thinking.

There are some other things. There's a marvellous sense of gratitude. It's so wonderful, isn't it? Everything! You just can't help laughing at it, you know? It's like a huge giggle.

The flip side of that is people taking everything so seriously, you know? *[laughs]*. I always think about making motor cars. They're just toys. That's all they are. We don't need cars. Yet we take the making of them so seriously. If you work for a car company, whether you've got the right car or not is a matter of life or death. They're just toys and yet we lose that sense of delight in them as toys. They're gorgeous. They're just beautiful toys. No wonder Krishnamurti loved blue cars. So there's a lot in it that's playful and it's very enjoyable and that's the lovely thing about it.

I'm always happy, even when I'm having a terrible day. Underneath I can always find my happiness. It's always there, all the time. The bedrock never changes. It's always one of tremendous peace and joy deep down, even though there might be lots of superficial froth and bubble going on. At times you might even identify with it for a bit and go with it and swing with it. Yet, in an instant, I can go back and reconnect with that sense of joy. When my nephew was killed, it didn't alter my joy and I knew everything was fine. It's very hard to talk about that because people think it sounds callous. That you were OK about your nephew dying. Yep. So – always – the joy is there.

❖   ❖   ❖

One of the teachers I spent quite a bit of time mucking around with years ago was a fellow called Da Free John. He was a very clever guy and a terrifically high grade teacher. He used to talk about the fact that you could always find the happiness in your body, you could always find it in your toes. It's always there. And at the time I wasn't sure I understood it, but later I totally understood it. You can always find your joy. Underneath everything, you are always happy. That is your prior condition. The sea is happy. It's at peace. It enjoys itself. It needs nothing. It's pretty happy with itself, actually. (*laughs*)

❖   ❖   ❖

I think I just wore out the other fella – the personality – eventually through effort. Got myself to the edge of the very edge where things can happen. And it just slowly dissolved. And it doesn't mean that it's not there available to you to be used. That's the lovely thing about it. It just means that you're not completely identified with it.

I mean, he's quite useful you know. No, he is. He's very clever, he's got good connections, he can do things, he can help people, he can help nature. My interest these days (to the extent that I want to do anything) is now about wanting to help nature. My identification with nature has grown stronger and stronger over the years. The sense of connection with nature is huge for me, in all the little things, and the sadness that comes with seeing nature being destroyed is also huge. And yet, that's all OK too.

Which doesn't mean it doesn't make me tremendously sad and upset, but it's just part of it. And that doesn't mean I don't get involved in trying to stop it either. I've been very involved in trying to stop logging of native forests in Victoria and I've been successful with that. I'm involved with an environmental organisation which is advising large companies on how to become sustainable and that's important too. People want either/or. They say: "Well, you shouldn't care – if you're an enlightened being! You shouldn't give a rat's arse about whether the planet's disappearing." It's not like that at all. It's both. No, it doesn't matter. Yes, I care. If you live in a world of opposites, that seems like nonsense. But I don't live in a world of opposites. It's all there, you know. It's all there at the one time. Everything.

❉   ❉   ❉

I think there is a type of transmission. We're all Buddhas. There is that part in all of us that we just haven't necessarily woken up. I think when you are with somebody who is perhaps a bit more aware, there's part of you that will identify with that. That part of you shines though very quickly, wants to come to the fore desperately, wanting to have a dialogue, wanting to express itself.

You get some very hard nuts who work very hard at stopping that from happening but, after a while, you see them laughing along with everybody else. I have a ball with people in meetings, just a hoot, and yet we're doing very serious strategy work, getting out difficult stuff. They often come out of a meeting saying: "Gee, that was fun, that was really enjoyable!" I have fun. We laugh a lot.

We want business to be so serious and I understand how serious it is. People's lives are at stake, their incomes, their jobs, their wellbeing. I understand that, but it's also not serious at all. It's funny, it's amusing, it's interesting, it's a game, it's a joke, it's enjoyable. If you lose your fear of making mistakes or failing and you trust in the process – the much bigger process that's just flowing, flowing, flowing, and you tap into that – I haven't gone wrong yet. I've been doing it for twenty-five years and it hasn't let me down once. It's not a bad endorsement.

The other day I was in New Zealand and I hurt my back lifting up some heavy timber. I wanted a massage and I heard there was a chap where we were staying who was very good. So I tracked him down and went to see him. He was a French guy, an older man in his seventies. I have no doubt that he was in that state. At the end of the massage, we walked out and we were looking at his garden. We didn't need to say a thing. There was nothing special about the level of communication at all, just an awareness. I knew that he was in a similar state and I think he knew that's where I was. So, no big deal. "Thanks very much. Bye. Au revoir." It's just no big deal.

There's that old joke: "When I find the secret of true wisdom, I'll let you know, if letting you know still seems to be important." (*laughs*)

❊　❊　❊

There's a Catholic theologian called Henry Nouwen. He came from a Christian and Catholic Jesuit perspective – nonetheless a great thinker and a wonderful being. He wrote a lovely little book called *Reaching Out*. He talked about the three movements of the spiritual life. The first movement was from loneliness to solitude. The second movement was from hostility to hospitality. The third movement was from illusion to prayer.

That's very beautiful. For some years I found it very helpful to work with those ideas. I never had a big problem with loneliness. I've never really been lonely. I did have a lot of trouble with hostility and hospitality, which is a huge test of how far you've travelled. And it took me a long time to understand the last one: the movement from illusion to prayer, the meaning of prayer. It's a whole of consciousness, whole of body surrendering to a life force. Being the sea is prayer.

❊　❊　❊

The boundaries are gone. And, in the dissolution of the boundaries, you're available, whereas you weren't necessarily available before. So much of your fuel was being used to work the C. engine. Keeping it all together, you know?

When you identify with the one who you really are you don't actually have a need to do anything because everything's just fine. Everything's just perfect. There's no need to get in the way, there's no need to worry and there's no need to struggle.

Ask yourself who's doing the pushing? Ask yourself who is the one who wants something to happen? Who is the one who wants something? Just be gentle to her, watch her. Don't be impatient with her. Every now and again ask yourself: "Who is the one who is anxious about this? Who is it? Who's there?" The question is also not so much: "Who is there?" but "Where? Where?" Try and locate that person. "Where is that person?"

It's beyond your power to move you forward. So trust in the process. Trust in the fact that everything's just fine. Don't give yourself a hard time. You're where you should be and if a feeling is still there, it's there for a reason. There's value in it as well.

From somewhere there is the thought that you are going to lose your very self in the process of surrendering. There's value in the integrity of the personality, in caring about your personality, in the integrity and conception of yourself. There is value in that. It's not as if it's all something to be got rid of. That's the thing, you know? You're not required to give up anything, but you think you are.

❊ ❊ ❊

the bean counter

T.F. I was born in an institution called *'St. Vincent's Asylum and Home for Unwed Mothers'*. I like saying this because it adds real drama to my story! I didn't always know, but I found out when I did genealogical research. My grandmother took me out of there and I was raised by my grandparents in a two-room flat in the city of Chicago. I knew my mother but I never knew my father. My mother would come and go.

It was a busy place, a fun place. I had three male cousins of the same age on the first floor of the flat with their mom and upstairs was me and my grandparents and my single uncle who lived there. I had a sister who was also born out of wedlock and put in a foster home, and she would come and go too. They put her in a boarding school. Although you could say: "That sounds terrible!" to me it had no meaning. The only thing I did as a kid was played. That was all that was required. There was no emphasis on education or anything in my house, just: "Don't bother us, go play." That was fine. We loved that.

At some point I remember going to school and the social dis-ease kicked in. You could relate it to the story of the earlier events but it just kicked in. The dis-ease, the discomfort in social settings and the sense of being a separate person was really pretty strong. It was a blue collar neighbourhood on the west side of Chicago and there was a sense of being an alien ... (*laughs*)

I *knew* I didn't belong there but I didn't know where I belonged. The blue collar environment was so overwhelming. I grew up as being a kind of shy alien ... (*laughs*) But I always enjoyed having fun, having experiences. Whether it was riding a motorcycle really fast or scuba diving or sky diving – all that kind of stuff was a fun part of my growing up.

I was shy with women, though. I didn't know how to do that at all. I was lucky some of them liked me and that made it easier. I never married. I don't have any children, but I never had a strong urge for that.

I became a drug user. I never became addicted but I used quite a lot of drugs, even the heavier stuff. I had a bad reaction and I went into acute anxieties. I think the medical term might be 'anxiety nervosis'. I didn't even have the mentality to see a doctor.

I lived with incredible anxiety. It was very physical. I could feel it in my arms, especially in my face so I found it almost impossible to smile. It took over my life. I could still go to work but it was really difficult being around people. Anxiety became the focus of my life.

I had a sense this would end and I could also see there were good days and bad days. As time went on, I even had this calendar where I would mark between one and a hundred what kind of a day it was. I could see that over time these anxieties were decreasing and I had a sense of moving in a direction where they were softening. I knew they would end.

That was, in a sense, the incredible beginning of

seeking – because I couldn't do anything else. I could work, and I had a relationship at the time, but all my energy was about these anxieties. Wanting peace became my focus of seeking. Other people will talk about 'wanting to become enlightened' or 'wanting to know the truth,' but 'peace' was the word that worked for me.

✻ ✻ ✻

Because I am more of a withdrawn person than an expan-sive person, it is very clear that I had nothing to do with the work I did. I really, literally, had nothing to do with it. I'll give you examples: After leaving school, I was working on the midnight shift in a factory that made bottle caps, but I didn't like it. I was hanging around the tavern, one of my friends suggested I go for an interview as a meter reader and I got that job. I never went back to my old job, I didn't even quit, I just didn't go back.

After five years I developed an interest in health and went to school to become a male nurse. A woman said: "There are plenty of nurses but they always need a respiratory therapist." I had no idea what it was but I became a respiratory therapist. After a couple of years I decided to go back to school and studied liberal arts.

Then I decided I needed a *real* job. I had a good head for num-bers, so I got a degree in accounting. Before I even graduated, I got a letter saying that the government was interviewing for a position as a revenue agent. I went to the interview not even caring about whether I got it or not – but I did.

So I'm a number cruncher, a bean counter – that's the historical phrase they use for accountants – I count beans all day. It's a perfectly meaningless job for me. A government bean counter is precisely the job you want if you are not career orientated and you just somehow get sucked into this spiritual consciousness thing.

✳   ✳   ✳

It was clear in my early life experience there was a sense of separation. I even viewed others as someone who I was dominant over or they were dominant over me. I thought in those terms. Then there was the recognition in my mid twenties that the bigger part of my problem was internal not external. So then what happened was what you might call a 'mini-shift' towards dealing with the internal drama as opposed to the external drama. But they were still there, the internal and the external.

My shift happened through 'A Course in Miracles' in July of 1993. I didn't know what happened but there was this incredible bliss. There was lots of laughing and lots of crying, which would alternate. It wasn't a sad crying. It was a release kind of crying. I am able to put it into words now.

Adyashanti would call the laughing and crying a 'by-product' of awakening. The words I would use now are, in addition to the 'by–products', there was this shift in consciousness, this expanded consciousness. In my case there weren't a lot of mystical experiences or anything but a tremendous amount of energy, a kind of catharsis and a sense of okayness – although I didn't use that word at that time.

Although fear didn't leave, fear was still there. Fear is my core story. Fear and the avoidance of fear were big elements in directing my life. Fear, for me, is a dis-ease in social environments. I can feel it in the body, the racing heart, a dryness in the mouth, a change in my voice. It was really strong and it would always be in the background for me. You might say that the fear was the real teacher because there was such identification with the image that was threatened by being afraid.

What happened to fear? It's still there but just as part of the landscape like a passing cloud, it arises and it subsides. What's different is the residual. Now it can arise and not necessarily have anywhere to stick. There is no feeling, no story. It's just pure emotion. It will maybe bounce around for a little while and then it will be gone.

✷　✷　✷

Anyway, there was this huge energetic impact on me. That all kind of spread out when the background became the foreground. At this time I had no idea what had happened and I wasn't involved with any people who knew about this kind of thing. The way I described it to some of my friends was that I was this dot in the space and then after the shift I was the space which contained the dot. I was still the dot but now I was also the space around the dot. I was in a state of blissful confusion, a state of not knowing. Then there was this tremendous energy to find out what was going on. I couldn't stop it. I just had to move towards this.

What was available for me at that time, as my shift had happened through 'A Course in Miracles', were the group meetings in the local Unity Church in Chicago, so I went there. But the feeling was not quite deep enough for me. It almost felt like a part-time thing for many of the people who were there and what had happened to me was a full-time thing.

It was huge. Everything was different. It was just constant. It didn't come and go. I would still go to work and everything was wondrous, just wondrous. Everything was easy, smooth and wondrous. I would go to work and then as work ended there was this energy arising.

Initially, I started running. After work I would go to the forest and I would run for mile or two until I was really tired. I would go to the local ice-cream shop, get a shake and drive home drinking it. I got hurt running so I started walking and then roller-blading everywhere. I was meeting new people through the 'Course in Miracles' and I got involved a little bit with the church.

Through the church I was introduced to a spiritual community in Wisconsin, where I met the full-time seekers. Someone called me up: "Can you do me a favour and pick up my friend at the airport? He's coming in from India. He needs a place to stay. Could you put him up for the night?" So I picked this fellow up. He had a deformed spine, a crooked back. He looked like someone from India, even though he was an American. I brought him home and he brought out these three pictures, one of Ramana Maharshi, one of Papaji and one of Sri Nisargadatta. He pointed to Sri

Nisargadatta and said: "I want you to get this guy's book. You need to read *I Am That*."

When I started reading *I Am That*, it was amazing. I couldn't wait to get home after my work, sit down and start reading it. I didn't understand it, but there was just something delightful that resonated. The whole Advaita world opened up to me.

I still had this sense of becoming and of having to *do* something until in 2000 I ordered *As It Is* by Tony Parsons – I was ordering everything at that time – and I read it. I said: "This is it. This is what I have always known." That was the end of seeking.

It wasn't the end of going to teachers and retreats. That still goes on and I enjoy it. What happens now for me is vacation and retreat together. It's a perfect combination for me. I love natural beauty. When the retreat is in an area where there is a lot of natural beauty there is a really strong pull for me to be there. There is just the enjoyment of being there in that environment.

That was the circle I had moved into. That was the end of becoming and any sense of me having any control over anything. There was the recognition that what gave me the sense of a personal 'me' was the sense of being able to become something, to choose, to direct things. That had all left.

So now the seeking was over but I still had these issues. My core story was still there, so there was an incongruency. There was nothing personal anymore but that wasn't reflected necessarily in my body or in my story. The sense of 'person,' of a personal person, was gone but the dis-ease was still there.

By this time I was surrounded by these radical non-dual teachers, including Joan Tollifson. There was this recognition that the shyness, the dis-ease, was part of it too. All of that is part of the oneness. It doesn't necessarily have to go the way you think it's going to go. It's just what it is and that includes everything. So my initial desire was for peace, and there has been a lot more peace in the conventional sense, but there is a peace beyond peace. That is the peace that allows even the core issues, the things that you think have to go – they are allowed also. That process, for me, is just ongoing and there is no sense that it has to end anymore, there's no fixation on that needing to end. You never get there. That's the joke. You can't fit through that keyhole. The 'you' is okay, it doesn't have to go anywhere. That sense that 'I haven't got it' or that there's still more to come is allowed too. That's part of it.

The idea that I had to be anything other than a human being who was afraid at times, who would be shy or have dis-ease, falls away. There is just this level of 'okayness' with whatever comes up.

❋   ❋   ❋

That's what's recognised – it was *always* there as a background thing that was completely ignored. It has no meaning, doesn't mean anything at all to the mind. That's why, when it's pointed to, it can't be found with the mind. If there is trying to find it with the mind, nothing happens. There may be intellectual understanding or frustration but usually there is just an ignoring of it and going into one's story. Then, for some reason (and it is a mystery to me) the background takes over. The background comes up and then there can be more relaxing, more peace, more okayness. I guess that can come and go. For me, the experience of expansion and contraction comes and goes, but the actual presence awareness doesn't go. Although it *could* go into a really small space.

For example: Before this I would have fantasies where I would do some wonderful thing and I would be the centre of the story as a hero-like character. Fantasies still arise but they arise only for a moment and when they are seen there is an inner smiling. The fantasy might be really interesting and so I might let it go on but from that point it doesn't have the same energy or impact so it tends to fall away. Then I go back to a more expanded sense of presence where I am more aware of myself and the surroundings, that kind of thing. The aperture then opens up a little bit. The contraction, in a prolonged sense, never came back for me.

It also has what Adyashanti calls the 'by-products'. There is more peace and the inter-personal relationships are much, much better. When there is okayness with you there can be recognition from the so-called 'other' that there is something going on. Then people come to you. There is a recognition. In my regular job, as a revenue agent for the Internal Revenue Service (IRS), I get surrounded by people who are deeply connected to their sad stories. They will come to me sometimes and we become friends. Some of the teaching may come up – but not so much now because I don't have to change their stories to the way that *I* see their story. I can just be with them with their story.

Also, synchronicity shows up more. It's kind of fun to see that but I don't put it together in any kind of cause or effect or as anything to strive towards. It's just part of the play of oneness. You could say that the closer you get to this oneness, the more you will pull in things around you, things flow better, more smoothly.

There is a real lightness about it. You recognise the impact of sayings like 'the lightness of being'. You recognise the lightness of it as being becomes the foreground. There's no longer the intense contraction, although that can happen too and then you are just having an intense contracted experience. The way I describe the manifestation, life as it is, is like having your hand in a vice. As you crank the vice and squeeze your hand it hurts like hell but when you let it up it feels really great. In order to get that great feeling you have to crank the vice down again. So there is this constant vacillating between contraction and expansion. The presence – the jewel – doesn't change. It remains in a contracted state or an expanded state. When you begin to give it qualities, you have to be very careful. That is why I would rather use the term 'by–products'.

This happened yesterday. I went with a couple of co-workers to dinner at a really nice restaurant at the top of a hotel. I was looking out of the window, enjoying the incredible view as the restaurant turned around. My co-workers started to talk about the other workers and the bosses – normal conversation for people who are really identified with themselves and the form. They wanted to know about my manager and so I began to tell them. There is a drama going on between me and my manager. It's much softer now but it is still an interesting story from the story point of view. So then I began to tell the story and they became really fascinated with the story. It had this evil character, my manager, and this nice person, myself, the victim. Then there is a realisation that the story is going into a place which does not feel good or natural. The story might subside, soften or even stop completely. It just goes back into softness.

The same thing is happening now. There is just something arising which says that this no longer feels right. While we are sitting here talking we have engaged the mind. That's the way this works. This dialogue involves engaging the mind and the memory and articulating in words, but what the teaching is pointing to is not what is going on here. It is pointing to what this is all happening in and it's going to be here when you shut down this microphone and leave, it's going to be here when you are going down the elevator and out through the door. That's what it's pointing to. The mind tends to look for it in the mind. When there was this recognition that there was no need to go anywhere else, that presence was basically *it*, the words that came to me were: "There is nothing here for the mind. This is just too ordinary." This is impossible to convey or to teach to some so-called 'other person' but we continue to try to do it. Then, for some unknown reason, we begin to rest in what is. The mind saying: "There has to be more," just becomes softer and softer. Once this has been seen clearly then you just talk about anything, it doesn't make any difference anymore. I spend a lot of time talking about the weather.

❊   ❊   ❊

Now that I've had this change, this shift, I resonate to the New Testament, to some of what Jesus said. Now I can hear it, where before the words were dead to me. Now there is life to some of the pithy aphorisms in the New Testament. They are really quite good, like: "The Kingdom of God is upon you now." You can't get much more present than 'now'.

❊   ❊   ❊

There is no story in being. If you ask, "What is being?" I can try to explain what it means to me but that is hard to do and actually futile. It seems to me that when you say things like 'being' or 'presence' or even the teaching 'I am' they really stop the mind. There is not much the mind can do with that. If I say, "Let's just *be* now for a moment," then the mind doesn't have anything to do. For me, doing is when there is a sense of: "We can make this different from what it is through some sort of will, determination or some sort of mind activity."

Generally the mind will see this as dull and boring but something can happen. I think that's why some people get addicted to meditation because they can go into presence very quickly and easily. There is expanded consciousness, peace and even bliss. But that is the confusion of the experience, the 'by-product' of the shift (expanded consciousness) and not the actual jewel.

I started meditating a long time ago, in my mid-twenties. I liked the feeling that I could attain, some peace and relaxation, from meditating. But then it would stop. It would come and go. There was a sense of value in meditating because it slowed down the mind and gave me this peace, but for me it never became big. I joined the meditation groups at the Shambhala Center, where I found a stronger resonance than with my regular circle of friends.

After meditation, I was always surprised that people would talk about how it felt to them, their experiences and reactions, what it brought up. To me, there was a sense that what was worth talking about was still here. It was there in meditation and it was still here. There was this aliveness here. For them, on or off the cushion, there was a separation. That was gone for me. It was full-time now. Everything was meditation.

It didn't matter whether you were in formal meditation or not. Meditation could *coincide* maybe with the big, permanent shift in consciousness, but then *anything* could, like walking down the street. So the focus on meditation became, for me, a distraction. I think that is the way it happens in many people's cases. The introduction to this whole 'consciousness' thing can, at any step of the way, be outgrown or it can become a distraction. Instead of meditation being the pointer it becomes what's pointed to. Then you become somebody who meditates, who goes into altered states.

❄   ❄   ❄

Last year, I went to Seattle to meet a friend and I had to go into hospital for an emergency cardiovert. We were supposed to be going away for the weekend to a really magical place. I went from that to being in this room surrounded by medical staff telling me that they were going to put me to sleep and cardiovert me. The sense of dying was there but it was fine. I don't want to say it was a wonderful experience but it was just an experience, there was a lightness to it. When I woke up, I asked: "When are you going to get this over with?" and my friend said: "It's over." Then I had a great weekend. Things just switched immediately.

There is just this okayness with whatever comes up, even the end of 'me'. In a sense, the end of 'me' already happened. The real end of me is the end of the personal 'me', the identification with 'me' who is somehow at odds with everything and needs to get everything in line, have things a certain way.

❄   ❄   ❄

I had a sense that this experience arose which was *incredible* and this presence arose which was totally ordinary. I also had a sense of the experience shrinking. I think what happens very often is that when the incredible experience shrinks or goes, the individual thinks they have lost something. They *have* lost something but they haven't lost presence.

They arose in me together and then this one *did* leave. My energy levels went down, I stopped running and my body just began to fall apart. It wasn't in any terminal way, but all sorts of aches and pains, back ache, knee ache, all that stuff. But by the time that happened, there was already the recognition that presence was the jewel so that falling away was not a big deal. And it comes back, too. There are days when the energy is high and there are no aches or pains. There are none now. I can identify with the experience coming and going.

What happens is that a lot of non-Advaita teachers are into re-creating the experience. That was big in the community I was in in Wisconsin. They were good at it. You would get in a circle and start jumping up and there was tremendous physical energy. The teacher would tell us to drink lots of coffee. People would go into altered states, there would be bliss and then they would come out of it. Very often they were miserable then and so would become addicted to the bliss experience.

❊   ❊   ❊

Presence doesn't come and go. It has always been here. But it has nothing for the mind. When those words come out and are expressed, the mind will say: "How can I get that?" Well, you can't get what you already have. It's incredibly full. There can't be any more. I have absolutely no investment in the future of this story in this body/mind. It would be nice if I was healthy and had a wonderful relationship and lived in the Pacific Northwest on Hillside with lots of money. That would be nice. But you can feel how that story drains away from presence.

There's always a story of how it is happening. But

stay in that place of not knowing. It's a natural place. It's a true place. It is like what Eckhart Tolle says: "That is the doorway." When you are at the doorway there is a sense of it being no big deal. I'm here and there is this presence, witnessing this and that. It's a bland place. Then you drop into some richness but I don't like to go there because the mind can grab that and start to seek it.

❊ ❊ ❊

The 'me' does arise and the core story is still here. If someone makes me feel small, for instance, I can feel defensiveness arising. But it is immediately seen. It's aerated. The core story is aerated and the 'me' is aerated.

The 'me' arose clearly when I came here in work–training with thirty other people. We are learning complicated material and we are all involved in taking tests. We can feel the competitiveness. Nobody wants to get the bottom score. Nobody wants to fail. Even if everyone passes, nobody wants to be the one who just made it. So I can feel the 'me' arising that is studying for these tests to get a good grade. It's *seen* but the energy still arises, the 'me' is still there and the 'me' is happy when it gets a good grade and is not so happy when it misses a problem. The 'me' does not want to be the worst or the best either. I just need to be in the middle, where I am not seen. My 'me' wants to just be comfortable in between the two polar opposites.

For some people the 'me' may have left. They use the word 'liberation' and I see that word as meaning that the 'me' has gone in terms of any reactivity.

They experience the preferences of the 'me' but any reactivity has gone. Perhaps that is what is meant by a liberated person? I don't know. What can leave, even before that happens, is a concern that you *have* to be liberated, that the 'me' has to leave. The 'me' can arise and that's just 'oneness me-ing'.

I was driving down the street one day and a young kid had been hit by a car. I am a trained respiratory therapist so I don't get too emotional about these things. I got out of the car and went up to the kid. When I was bending over the boy I found that tears started running down my face but there wasn't a personal sense about it. There was this moment of pain. His dad was there too and he was in emotional pain. There was this sense of identification with the sad story of the moment and then it stopped. I went away from there and it stopped. It wasn't anything that I turned on or off.

It may not happen like that another time. This is part of what is arising in your story. It may include sadness and tears and it may include more of that now because there's no longer any separation as there was before. But it is no longer as big either. In a sense, you can be more helpful. There is no investment in 'What happened here?' and 'Who's right or wrong?' or 'This is a really awful thing.' The need to have anything any other way just doesn't have much energy anymore.

❊ ❊ ❊

It's all happening naturally. I would say that if you look at the first instance of your desires or aversions then you will see that they arise from nowhere. Our desires and aversions arise from nowhere. For example: I have an abandonment issue because my mother left me in an orphanage. That's a story that arose from another story. If you go back to my mother's circumstances, if you trace things back, they just arise from nowhere.

No matter where you think your aversions and desires came from – whether they came from you, your personal inadequacies or your parents or your grandparents or the government – if you trace it back to the beginning you will see that they arose from nowhere.

My progressive political tendencies come from nowhere. I came from the west side of Chicago, from a blue collar neighbourhood. They didn't have political progressiveness. It just arose in me. There is no need to find out where any of this arose. The only thing that this is pointing to is right here, right now and what is arising now.

❋   ❋   ❋

The simple little things become rich. Sitting here in the evening, looking out of the window and watching the birds. They fly around in flocks. It becomes really rich as nothing becoming something. There is a richness to it that the mind can see as completely bland and uninteresting.

Every time I try to describe it I have to refer to words that are experiential. It just doesn't seem like they work. There's just a profound okayness. A wonderfulness.

That includes the negative parts too. The sadness. That manifests also and you have to include it all, all of the experiences. It's an extraordinary ordinariness.

nature's spiritual, but so is a teaspoon

K.N. So, you need my name and my age and the fact that I'm ordinary? Yep, that's fine. (*laughter*). I'm K., I'm in my mid fifties and I work as a nurse in England.

I'd been on a so-called spiritual path for twenty odd years, and my teacher taught non-duality in this Upanishadic or Vedantic sense. I always felt non-duality was the important part of his message, although other people preferred the miracles and the flashy bits. At the group meetings I was always slightly frustrated it wasn't the bit people were interested in.

I was a very lazy meditator. I would do almost anything rather than meditate. I wasn't good at it. I used to like doing things like watching telly – and yeah! – mucking around and not doing much and telling jokes. I became increasingly bored really, not in any high idealistic sense, but I was a bit cheesed off after being totally committed to these teachings for quite a long time.

Then I had a dream in which the teacher appeared to me at a function and said: "Take a back seat.

Concentrate on other things". This was remarkable, considering the tradition from which he came. So I immediately stopped being the leader of the group and stopped following him and felt: "There's a sort of space in my life." In view of how dedicated I'd been in a lazy sort of way, I didn't really care, which again was remarkable.

❊   ❊   ❊

I had something that I could probably call an 'experience' a couple of times previously. Way back at a retreat, I had what seemed like one. It was as if – if you've ever played a violin or any musical instrument, you can put a mute on it – and it was like a mute had been put on something that was K. There were a few hours where there wasn't a K. I still don't know if that was a state or a foretaste or what it was. In fact, that doesn't matter.

By a long series of coincidences, I happened to pop into a Tony Parsons talk in Glastonbury. About half way through, I knew that what he was saying had actually hit the spot. It did that boring thing called 'resonating' and what was really great is that you didn't actually have to do anything – which made me slightly suspicious – but I just couldn't keep away from going to his meetings. Although it seemed like a progression, don't be misled into thinking that there's any linear progression or anything like that in this business! Do not be misled into thinking there is a progress or a process or that you can go from being unenlightened to being enlightened. Forget it. But in the story of our lives, it seemed that there were links and causes.

✳   ✳   ✳

One August in Hampstead, about two years ago, I was sitting down listening to Tony Parsons. On the train up to London that day, I thought I wanted to ask a sort of 'showing off' question. I was going to ask: "Sense of self seems very vague. Has anything changed? There's a sort of vagueness about this K. thing." Then I forgot the question. I was just listening to Tony and following it in quite a relaxed way, without trying to be relaxed. Then, when I stood up at the end of the talk, it was all different. Everything had changed.

I wasn't quite sure what had happened when I stood up, but when I went out – it was a moderately sunny day – I really wanted just to be alone. I couldn't work out what I felt like. And I wasn't prepared for the clichés – lots of light and glory. It wasn't quite glory, but the light was absolutely dazzling for about half an hour. I thought it was just myself, not being accustomed to the sun, but it wasn't that at all. It really is indescribable – like something had broken or something had died, although it was an intense aliveness. And then comes silence, because it can't be described.

It's not a state. There is a body/mind called K. which trots along and does all its usual things, but there's this all-encompassing thing that is 'no thing' that's always there. So it's not a state. It sometimes feels a bit like a state, like when I stood up and went for that walk in the sunshine – that was a bit state-like – but it's *not* a state.

It's going to be very disappointing when I talk about the light, because at the time I just thought that there

101

was an awful lot of light around and I wasn't used
to the sun, so I was squinting a bit. That didn't seem
to help and there just seemed to be light everywhere
– but I didn't think it was anything to do with the way
I thought the person that was me was feeling. It wasn't
really a grand experience. With hindsight, that's how
it was – like using the physical memory to remember
something that you can't remember with the physical
memory – but Hampstead doesn't contain that much
light normally.

✳   ✳   ✳

It's that suddenly everything changed, and yet
everything was exactly the same. Something came
forward and something else receded. And once I got
there, I knew I couldn't go back – although I was
actually in the same place that I'd never left.

Reading the literature and listening to people, you
probably would call it 'awakening' or 'liberation', but
really there are no words for it, which is very irritating,
if you happen to be doing a book about it.

The 'you-ness' is sort of there. It doesn't vanish
in a blaze of glory and you're suddenly perfect. In
Hampstead, with all this light everywhere, as I was
talking and listening to people, indeed, the thoughts
were going on. I was thinking: "This is such an amazing
thing. I've got to pretend to be normal" (*laughter*).
And that's the best way I can describe it. Then it just
becomes normal. The 'you-ness' was thinking: "Oh, I
must pretend to be normal." Everything had changed,
but the 'you-ness' went on, the K. went on, doing all the
things that K. did. Any old habits – like trying to please

people and trying to be popular – it doesn't stop.

Liberated and awakened ... I always thought that when whatever it was that appeared to have happened at that time happened, I would rush out and long to teach people. I like talking to people and being enthusiastic about things and I thought: "I can really help people to understand what this is like" – but I can't even tell the difference between awakening and liberation. I can't even give a proper name to this, whatever it is. I have to use other people's words. All I can say is: "Something has gone forever and something that's always been here is still here, and although everything has changed, everything's the same, and this moment ... " and there she trails into silence.

I can't experience this K-ness because there isn't a me to experience it. Otherwise you're falling into a process whereby you witness yourself, which is useful if you need to sort out your psyche – if you're unhappy and you want to be happier – but I'm not witnessing myself. There may be something witnessing, but it's all part of the one and you can't separate it out. Witnessing makes it sound as if there's a separation and there really is no separation. That's probably the best way of saying it.

I don't feel a shining oneness with every object that I appear to see, which is a shame really and very disappointing for people reading this. But there's something that permeates everything and that *is* everything. So although the senses perceive the coffee cup and they perceive the microphone and they feel the warmth of the stove, at the same time ... this is really quite difficult ... all these things are the one and they're part of the one and they're not different. The senses still do their thing, which is to see things as separate, because that's how your senses operate. They can't suddenly change. But there is this awareness that isn't the senses. Perhaps the difference between now and ten years ago is that the awareness is right in the front and the sense bit is still there, but it's taken its place where it belongs. That isn't a brilliant summary. This is why I'm glad I didn't rush off to be a teacher, because I wouldn't have been a good one.

One of the ways to try and describe it is it's like a sort of living, vibrating, interested, alert 'something' that permeates absolutely everything and is everything and – you know, in fact, that it's always been there. One of the things is there's that feeling almost of a 'watcher', so at one time there was a sort of feeling of this awareness, almost like something holding its breath, and this intense aliveness, and now I guess that that aliveness isn't separate, not that it ever was separate. So yes, the senses are seeing the coffee cups, they're hearing the hiss of the gas stove and that's what senses are for! That's fine! It's just part of the story, but the other thing is deeply embedded in everything. It *is* everything.

All the clichés are dreadfully, dreadfully true. When you say: "I am that", it really is true, which is extraordinary because I'd mouthed that in Sanskrit and Hindi for twenty-five years and thought very seriously: "I am that. I am God. I am not different from God." Indeed I'm not – but it's not quite what I meant at the time.

With hindsight, it was always there. I can see it – as far back as a little girl being bullied at school and sitting on a snowy step – I can see it. It was there. That dreadful teenage crush – I remember teenage crushes – and the awful insecurity of the early twenties – but it was there all along. It was still there. Now I can see it, or should I say, now it is seen.

I wasn't feeling it. This is hindsight, because time sort of vanishes *and* it's there, because perception of time is a bit like a sense. From that point of view, I know it was there. But the thing that thinks it is K., the thing that thinks it's 'I', in inverted commas, the thing that thinks it is doing things, the thing that thinks it has a crush, the thing that thinks it's being bullied, the thing with a cold wet bottom sitting on a step – that thing cannot, by its very limitations, actually understand the totality.

The real thing that is difficult (except it's not difficult) is that there is something inside so many of us that screams with fear at the thought of dying. Something died on that day in August. And it was fine. But prior to that, there were many moments of fear.

From the age of about five I had these episodes of disassociation where I knew I wasn't K. and they were really, really scary. And it's taken, well, fifty years for them not to be scary.

I knew I wasn't me but there was a sort of void which was very frightening. These experiences would come upon me – they seemed like experiences – and there was no warmth or joy to them. They were cold and frightening. I didn't know who I was. It wasn't psychotic, although I sometimes wondered if it was.

That sort of fear never properly left me until that day in August.

I think that's a useful point for many people. There is a fear, and it's a fear of death, because it's as if part of you dies. That's what you think at the time. But in fact, it's fine, no need to be frightened, it's great. But I was scared for years and years because the whole way you define yourself and your existence is deeply threatened and for some reason you think that it matters, but it doesn't.

There's a thing, or there was a thing for many years that called itself K., and it thought it had some control over both itself and other people and that it was an entity that existed separately. That entity has some sort of vested interest I suppose, in continuing, it doesn't want to be shoved in the background to just toddle along quietly without anyone getting terribly excited about it, and have all attention removed from it, so I guess it's a fear of dissolution. Perhaps death is rather a hard word. But people do talk about dying, it all makes it sound rather too dramatic though and we're not into huge drama here. I always remember Tony Parsons saying that I'd be very cross with him because it was such a simple thing – it's such an easy, quiet thing. I wasn't cross with him, but he's right.

I boringly say this every time: "Everything has changed, but nothing has changed." And so the K. thing toddles along, does all its usual stuff, doesn't like loud noises, doesn't like waiting in queues, fond of dogs, all the things that identifies it as K., those things still go on. But I suppose the identification has gone. That doesn't mean there isn't swearing when stubbing the toe or in domestic arguments. Let me assure you that this does not signal the end of marital strife or all the things that are the opposite of marital strife – which are all the nice things that we won't go into in detail here ... (*laughter*).

I'm not sure how it affects relationships, I mean fortunately my husband is very much into this – there's an old-fashioned term! – and it was he who suggested I went to see Tony Parsons in the first place, because I happened to be in Glastonbury. So it's all his fault. (*laughter*) He's only taunted me once so far – and he's still alive to tell the tale! – saying he expected better of me, considering what had happened. At the same time he says there *is* a difference but I haven't got any tidier in the house, I must say, and I'm not a better housekeeper. Probably slightly easier to live with, in some other respects, but it's not a recipe for anything, and I guess there might be problems if the partner wasn't interested at all. You still enjoy the things you used to enjoy. Some of them even more, so that's the good news. Other things occasionally lose their flavour. It's difficult to tell if that's just progress of years or whether it's due to what appeared to happen.

But some things are certainly more enjoyable. I'm not a major chocolate addict, but in fact I can savour a square of chocolate in a far more interesting way than I used to be able to – it's a mystery to me why. The converse is that I always used to feel very 'spiritual' when walking out in the countryside. I used to feel I had this 'spiritual' connection with nature. And that's gone. I do feel much better if I go for a walk in the countryside and I do enjoy it and I feel much better afterwards – it obviously does me good physically – but I don't have the same 'spiritual' connection with nature. Perhaps it's because it was a slightly self-conscious spiritual connection because nature's spiritual, but then so is a teaspoon. That slightly self-indulgent spirituality has gone. I still enjoy going for those walks, but it's different.

I was just going to add something about spirituality because I did feel in years gone by that although I was a very lazy meditator I was a deeply spiritual person and that really made me quite special. And I always remember way back, I was sharing a room with someone in India in the 1970's and instead of saying 'I' she referred to herself as 'this body'. She would say: "This body is hungry," and I was deeply impressed. I really wished I was that sort of person. That feeling stayed with me for many years but I'm glad to say it's gone now and I'm not a spiritual person.

You can really quite indulge those things that you felt slightly guilty about doing as a spiritual person – like watching television. I really really enjoy watching some rubbish television now and there's a sort of freedom in the enjoyment because I don't feel that I've got to be a better person or a spiritual person.

Then there is also this question of ethical behaviour and that really remains a deep mystery to me. I still have the feeling that if I see someone in trouble I want to help them and if I see someone who keeps getting into trouble, who's got the sort of problems that are cyclic, I just get a bit bored with it and can't be bothered to help them anymore. Which is a sort of normal human reaction so that hasn't changed, but some feelings seem to be much deeper in a weird sort of way, they're much more poignant. I cry more often at television, which is quite embarrassing, and then the feeling's gone. I can't explain that either but it seems to be a feeling that's less tied up with all sorts of other stuff, it comes and goes, it passes like the weather. I would say that quite a lot of it is still a mystery to me. So don't think you're going to understand everything and know everything.

* * *

I couldn't go back because all there is is this. And the thing that thinks it's liberated, it just ain't so: "This is all there is. And that's all there is." There's no liberation and there's no no-liberation. There's no bondage and there's no freedom. But there are clichés and I've just repeated most of them (*laughter*).

Here's something to add. I think I may be a more boring person now because I used to really feel that I should be the life and soul of the party, not that I like parties, but I can be witty on a good day and I can't always be bothered now. I do enjoy my own company more, I could sit quietly for a long time but I could equally go shopping, drink a glass of wine, so don't start thinking it's a spiritual thing, please. But I guess I am slightly more boring.

So what is it that's so compelling about this liberation or awakening or change or whatever you like to call it? Why should anyone be interested even? Indeed it's a mystery. But it really is a sort of freedom and we can only use words that are clichés but it does set you free in a way, although you were always free and you didn't know it.

If you are seeking, this is what you are seeking. But seeking won't get you there and this is the paradox.

I'm trying to make this accessible. So it *is* what I was seeking and yet it's completely different. Because all the time it was there and it didn't need to be sought. I was the thing I was seeking. When I was a seeker, I thought that a lot of the things (like calming the mind, not feeling angry, not spending money, not watching telly, chanting mantras) would not only make me a better person but would make me happier. I think that's what I wanted. But I also thought they would hopefully lead to liberation. They certainly *don't* lead to liberation. They can make you happier but they won't give you what you seek.

I have to keep reiterating that the light after the meeting that August was meaningless. It's still a bit of a mystery to me. I wouldn't say the light goes on and certainly it doesn't seem like that any more. I think it's just integrated. Some people do see a lot of light but I don't, I don't think it means anything either way but I guess it permeates everything. It's like poison gas and once the gas is released you can never escape it.

What will happen I guess, though it's different for everyone, is that your personal life story will go on and it will seem as if things are happening which lead you to awakening or to the dropping away of the self or whatever you like to call it and it seems like that and it certainly seemed to me as if going to Tony Parsons' talks really helped stuff drop away. But as there's no time how could that be? All there is is this one thing in the constant play of forms, and here we are in the play.

I could say that in the years past there was a perpetual dissatisfaction, knowing that something wasn't quite right and always seeking and grasping, thinking things weren't right or they should be better. And I would say now that most of that dissatisfaction has gone; there's still the story where you'd like to earn a bit more money or you'd like to have the perfect haircut, it's not really terribly significant, it's just part of the K. thing. But that perpetual dissatisfaction has gone. I would say this is the way you can truly be yourself, where you can be at ease with yourself and at ease with the world. It doesn't mean that you'll like the things you didn't like or that you'll hug people who have body odour, or anything like that, but there is a sense of ease of naturalness, of being truly yourself, not being pulled every which way by all the competing demands of what you think are outside influences and cultural norms and spiritual values.

This is an example from work: I'm a union representative, I was representing a union member in what was quite a difficult situation and I just felt able to be myself. I obviously had to be professional, but I felt that it was just the way it was. I didn't have to agonise about the way I should seem to be. And that sounds quite small to some people, but I felt that I was integrated. I suppose that it really is the ultimate integration of all those things that you thought were separate. So there isn't really a conflict between what you thought was spirituality, what you thought was personal life and what you thought was work life. *Integration* is quite a good word.

I'm sure I'm not original in saying this, but one of the fears is that you'll lose what made you an individual. We would lose the essence of what made us – in this case, that my K-ness would go and how sad that would be. Quite often we're scared of that for a long time – not everyone – but the really gorgeous thing is that you can be *more* yourself.

One extra for me is that I really do feel more totally and joyfully myself in situations where previously I wouldn't have done. I feel more spontaneous. I wouldn't say that there aren't awkward situations, but there is an inner authority. There is a feeling that everything's okay and I don't have to rush around pleasing everyone.

Printed in the United Kingdom
by Lightning Source UK Ltd.
131930UK00001B/99/P